*Applause for **Above the Clouds: 9 E***

My friend, Michael Blackwell, has captured the essence of what true _____
in life. His "9 Essentials" (my favorites include Achievement, Spirituality, Legacy)
are inspiring, informative and blend strong advice with good-natured humor.
As a major religious visionary who leads North Carolina in educating and helping
children, Michael combines theological insight with practical application
to produce this eagerly-awaited volume. Five stars!

James B. Hunt, Jr.
Governor of North Carolina – 1977-1985; 1993-2001

Michael Blackwell has thrived among the peaks over an estimable career. He has
built an ongoing remarkable life as minister and master communicator, husband and
father, non-profit executive, role model, and altogether wondrous guy. ***Above the
Clouds*** explains how to do this... and keep doing it. You will be inspired and
motivated by this treasure of a book.

Curry Kirkpatrick
Former Writer, Editor and Broadcaster
Sports Illustrated, Newsweek** and **ESPN

Excuses for not exercising? There are none, Dr. Blackwell says, and he has
convinced me that maintaining one's health is imperative in pursuit of one's
life goals. He relates, with humor, his own struggles with putting on the pounds
and confesses how some subversive brownies foiled his intent to parade a 100-
pound weight loss in front of folks he wanted to impress. Well. I'm impressed!
You might be, too.

Karen L. Parker
Former Career Newspaper Copy Editor
Member of NC Journalism Hall of Fame

Above the Clouds – and its "9 Essentials" – is inspiring, luminous, and at times,
laugh-out-loud funny. Michael writes with poignancy and vulnerability. A sizzling
read and captivating gift that I will share with friends, family, and colleagues.

Sharon Allred Decker
Chief Operating Officer, Tryon Equestrian Center

Continued...

Once again, the charismatic Dr. Blackwell puts into clear and concise words – with life-changing experiences and dramatic illustrations – the keys to peak performance that he's been proclaiming for the last 50 years. **Above the Clouds** is an essential read for anyone who wants to live life to its fullest.

Marian Phillips
Founder, Leadership North Carolina

Losing 101 pounds – and keeping it off – is no easy task. Dr. Blackwell shares his three secrets (and personal struggles) in the Health chapter of **Above the Clouds**, one of nine essentials for thriving at the peak. I'll gladly recommend the book to my patients and to anyone who desires optimum health for optimal living.

P. Ray Morrow, Jr., M.D.
Assistant Professor of Medicine, Wake Forest Baptist Health

Touchdown! **Above the Clouds** is THE CATCH of this season. . .and every season. The book is both entertaining and exhilarating. My lifelong friend has penned a masterpiece.

Dwight Clark
Former National Football League Player, San Francisco 49ers' #87 (number retired)
Two Super Bowl Championships

Choose your personal Essential for "thrive at the peak" performance – Purpose, Laughter, Relationships (or one of the other six) – and you'll be immediately transformed to a world of "dreams can, indeed, come true." **Above the Clouds** will kick-start your life toward a new level of success and satisfaction. I guarantee it!

Ty Boyd – CSP, CPAE
International Motivational Speaker
Co-founder of Ty Boyd Executive Learning Systems

Without a doubt, the best book ever by the BEST BOPPY EVER.

Gabriella and Piper
The Author's Granddaughters

★

Also by Michael C. Blackwell

New Millenium Families
A Place for Miracles
UpsideDown Leadership
Riches Beyond Measure

An additional book of interest

Just Call Me Mickey:
From Mill Town to Mills Home,
the Journey of Michael C. Blackwell
by Wint Capel

Above the Clouds

9 Essentials for Thriving at the Peak

by Michael C. Blackwell

BCH PRESS
Thomasville, North Carolina

Above the Clouds – 9 Essentials for Thriving at the Peak

ISBN 978-0-9979252-0-3

Printed in the United States of America

Art Direction; Cover & book design: Jim Edminson
Illustrations & sketches: Darin Rhue & Michelle Hanks
Photos: Jennifer Westmoreland & Fotolia by Adobe

BCH PRESS: *www.bchfamily.org/bchpress*

DEDICATION

Paul Hunt Broyhill

Paul Broyhill has been a friend,
mentor and confidant since 1983.
His words – *PUSH AHEAD* – are words
I repeatedly lean on when making
tough decisions or casting new visions.
At age 92, Paul is still "at it." I draw
strength from his entrepreneurial spirit
and relentless pursuit of excellence.
Thank you, Paul Broyhill, for your
shining example of leadership
and true friendship.

Contents

★

★

Acknowledgments

Collaborative joy is always part of writing a book.

Jennie Counts, my assistant for over 25 years, has been part of all my books, speeches, dreams, and visions for Baptist Children's Homes of NC, and all endeavors in which I've played a part. She's smiled through every re-write, kept meticulous files of the ever-changing manuscript, and has been an uplifting spirit throughout this process. As always, thank you, Jennie.

Norman Jameson and Jim Edminson have taken words and concepts and turned them into soaring commentary and design. I've worked with them for many years and they know my passion for effective communication. Thanks, guys.

A number of people read and critiqued the manuscript. Karen Parker, a friend from college and award-winning copy editor, was unrelenting in her honorable criticisms. Anne McCracken, a friend from high school, made sure I kept "me" in proper context. Bob Denham, prolific author, retired Professor of English, and my brother-in-law, offered helpful suggestions. They all spent many hours in conversation with me about the

★

true nature of **Above the Clouds**.

I asked numerous colleagues to read the Spirituality "essential." It's amazing what differing views they offered. Thank you: Bill Boatwright, Tony Cartledge, Doug Cole, Tom Denton, David Smith, Clay Warf, Ed Beddingfield, Kathy Blackwell, Randy Sherron, Joel Campbell, Nancy Hege, and Martha McDowell.

Darin Rhue and Michelle Hanks provided sketches and illustrations for this book and future projects. Creativity knows no bounds with these two.

The Broyhill Family Foundation has generously assisted me with all my books – this one included – and many other endeavors. Shelia Triplett-Brady, Executive Director of the Foundation, is a superb writer and motivational speaker and is Personal Assistant to Paul Broyhill, Chairman of the Foundation. It is my personal joy to dedicate this book to Mr. Broyhill, who has always soared above the clouds in making Broyhill Furniture a household name and whose many entrepreneurial visions have made this world a better place in which to live.

It's my fondest hope that all who read **Above the Clouds** will do just that: never be content with "average" or plain vanilla, but be inspirited to explore the heights, dream big dreams, and squeeze every good thing from the few brief moments we have on life's daunting stage.

Michael C. Blackwell
Thomasville, North Carolina

Foreword

Above the Clouds. . .is not merely a philosophical or spiritual tome that will keep your head in the clouds. Rather, my dear friend, Dr. Michael Blackwell has written a book that is God-conscious, personal and grounded in what I refer to in Vocal Awareness as Spiritual Pragmatism.

This is a book that takes you on a **journey** to achieving personal **mastery**. Many authors write books on a purpose-driven life which are often only linear or theoretical. Michael lives his life not self-consciously but always conscious of Self–Source. It is reflected in the intimacy and clarity of his writing.

If you were to hear him speak, the very sound of his sonorous voice energetically compels you to action, encouraging you to risk while at the same time helping you feel safe, secure and enveloped through the trust and integrity reflected in his beautiful voice. For you see, Michael is the embodiment of the **work** he teaches. Through the wonderful storytelling web he weaves, Michael reveals **HimSelf**, and in turn, will help you discover your **DeeperSelf**.

★

As I teach in Vocal Awareness, we cannot empower another person, but we can help that person empower themselves. That is exactly what Michael does in this wonderfully insightful book as he becomes your tour guide enabling you to "thrive at the peak."

Arthur Samuel Joseph, M.A.
Founder of Vocal Awareness™
President, Vocal Awareness Institute, Inc

Above the Clouds

*9 Essentials for Thriving
at the Peak*

INTRODUCTION

Few are Born to the Heights.

Yet the peak compels us. The sky-piercing boldness of a mountain's highest point continually draws upward the eyes of those who live beneath. The peak's snow-blanketed shoulders catch morning's first light, while the city below lies in shadow.

Peak weather is different and difficult. Brutal winds assail the pinnacle, pelting it with snow even in summer.

The tallest peaks stand bald and bold in defiance of harsh sun, vicious storms, fierce wind, thin air, and conditions so harsh that no vegetation will grow above a certain elevation. That tree line, easily visible to those on the plateau, marks the highest elevation to which one could aspire to live on that mountain.

If we ever are to dwell there, at the peak, we must learn not only to climb, but then also to thrive at the top.

★

I am 74 years old as I write this, and my table sits on my little rock outcrop on the peak I now call home. I haven't been here long—it took me 40 years into my career and 33 years as president of the Baptist Children's Homes of North Carolina to arrive at that place in my life when—with a firm grip on the boulders around me—I can look over the vast valleys and plains of my journey and realize that I'm finally here. I'm fully engaging all the tools, gifts, skills, experience, education, failures, and relationships of my travels, and it feels great.

To be at the peak is fulfilling, gratifying, energizing, spiritually satisfying, and thrilling in such a deep and broad way that sometimes I just shake my head and say a word of thanks that I've arrived in this place while I yet live.

Because it is so gratifying and rare, and because it took me so long to get here, I am writing to mark some trails for you. This book shares nine broad areas of life— **the essentials**—that if you pay attention to them now, they will help you traverse, arrive and thrive at your peak sooner than I did.

Still, reaching the peak is not the final step. Many people have clamored and climbed to reach their peak and then fallen off. I think immediately of Richard Nixon, O.J. Simpson and any number of flash-in-the-pan, one-hit-wonder entertainers.

Your ultimate success that will fill you with deep, soul-nurturing satisfaction is not simply

★

reaching the peak: Success is learning to thrive above the tree line, to run the ridges with the ibex, to continue living, learning and succeeding at your highest level — whatever level that is — until your journey is complete.

The Alpine ibex is an uncannily agile mountain goat that can leap from one rock sliver to another, as writer Ellen Meloy said in **Eating Stone**, "with nothing beneath their hooves but air and a foothold barely larger than my lower lip."

Video from astounded tourists shows a group of ibex casually licking the salt and minerals from near the top of the almost-vertical wall of the Cingino Dam in Italy. It's been said an ibex hooves are like flypaper. Those unique hooves are split and spread under their own weight, broadening their ability to clutch the smallest rock and giving them what seems like supernatural sticking power.

To live on the peak, you almost need supernatural sticking power.

It took me 30 years to reach the place where I can survey life below the tree line with a sense of satisfaction and accomplishment, where I thrive sure-footed and agile enough to avoid predators and forage successfully without fear.

For me the question remains — and I offer it for your personal consideration no matter where you are — what do I need to be doing here at this point in my life?

★

"Career" does not begin to encompass the scope of that question. I'm talking about life on the peak. I'm at the point where there is little separation between career and life, between what I do and who I am. Oddly enough, that's not the negative I might have thought it to be when I was younger.

Don't think I'm affirming a person who pursues career over life, or prefers colleagues over a significant other.

I'm talking about an essence of living, a unified present, a gurgling stream of life in which waters flow over the various rocks that create its stream bed, each an element of my life: family, job, church, spirit, career, vacation, health, recreation, friends, goals and dreams.

Yes, my dream machine hasn't run out of bubbles just because I'm approaching 75.

And that is a significant part of life at the peak: dreams keep us afloat, they keep our feet sticking to impossibly narrow ledges—and they empower us to brave the elements and find those sparse morsels that will sustain us.

Here's to life at the peak—and to running the ridge together.

★

PURPOSE

No. 1

Seeking mastery
of where your passion
points you

★

CHAPTER 1

Embracing a Journey of Discovery

Did you emerge from your mother's womb destined for a certain and single purpose? Is your ultimate measure of a successful life how nearly you identify and live that purpose?

Or have you surveyed the vast array of possibilities, picked a destination, and headed directly for it? Or have you simply said, "Life is a journey" wherever the rails take me: the wind in my face relishing each moment, anticipating the excitement of every hill climb, curve, and clickity-clack.

I've never felt my life was a game board and that birth landed me on the "start" block at the beginning of a multicolored road leading to a destination I could reach only if I rolled the dice the right number of times and sent other contestants back to the beginning if I landed on their space.

And yet.

I do believe that an attentive life will follow

a direction that fits your personality and natural gifts. Your ultimate vocational or life expression could be any number of different things. It's likely that the "job" you are in now, and certainly the one to which you aspire, didn't exist in its current form back when you were wondering what you wanted to be when you grew up.

Let's not confuse career with purpose: Your life is bigger than your career. If you are simply dedicating your waking hours to career to the neglect of your spirit, family, health, and healthy interests, you won't find your purpose, no matter what career goals are reached. Following internal passion leads you to purpose.

Still, we tend to think of our lives as what we "do." And for many of us, our career defines what we "do."

Purpose evolves as our heart's passion evolves. The magnetic lodestone of purpose that you felt drawing you forward when you were younger may have shifted poles by now. Maybe you trained for and achieved that early purpose, but you've grown beyond that role and you're looking for "next." Instead of wondering if you've missed your purpose, realize that purpose can change as you grow and evolve.

I will use my own story as an example of such evolution.

Was I born to be president of Baptist Children's Homes of North Carolina for the past 33 years?

★

I don't know. What I do know is that from my earliest years I wanted to learn more about the world and to lessen the suffering of children.

That desire and interest was further fueled by my church's involvement with Baptist Children's Homes. We received their newspaper **Charity & Children**. We collected an offering every year to support their work and gladly heard Children's Homes' speakers when they made their rounds, updating churches about their service to children.

Early on I thought my purpose was to be a news broadcaster and radio personality. That's what I loved, and opportunities came my way as I gravitated toward responsibilities that had me setting up the film projector in junior high school, making announcements over the intercom, emceeing a show, or giving a speech for a special event.

Eventually, I was in charge of the talent show. I did the play-by-play announcing for the local American Legion baseball team. I was not on the basketball court and I never played football, but I was at every game because I called them and I traveled with the band.

I always thought it was cool that I got to do those things. My voice became very familiar to folks in my area, and each of those opportunities solidified my sense that broadcasting was in my future.

I followed that yearning and those affirmations in high school to host "Mickey's Record Shop" on the local radio station. At UNC Chapel Hill I majored in journalism and wrote for the *Daily Tar Heel*. I was totally wrapped up in the newspaper, probably to the detriment of my classroom performance.

Being on a major national campus in turbulent times, I skipped class to get to Washington and cover John F. Kennedy's funeral. UNC President William Friday was a friend and mentor who encouraged me.

President Friday graciously went out of his way to introduce me to important political figures who came to campus, such as Lyndon Johnson, Dean Rusk and Adlai Stevenson, the American ambassador to the United Nations.

I'm still embarrassed that upon meeting Stevenson, who was primed to be interviewed by a reporter from the *Daily Tar Heel*, my piercing and insightful first question was, "So, how are things at the U.N.?"

Following graduation, I worked for a newspaper in Durham and radio stations in Raleigh and Charlotte. Had I discerned, and was I pursuing and achieving my purpose?

Apparently not, because I started to feel a yearning for what seemed to me a larger purpose — applying my talents to the burgeoning work of the Southern Baptist Convention's Radio and Television Commission.

I figured having a seminary education and some experience as a minister would broaden my qualifications for ministry through broadcasting.

★

So, even as a new husband, I anchored the news on television at night and was a youth minister at a Raleigh church, all the while finishing seminary to prepare me for my next purpose.

Life was a blur, and as I relate later, I didn't take good care of myself during this time. But I was striving to achieve my next goals, even if I wasn't ready to identify them as my "purpose."

Over time, Southern Baptists' level of commitment to the Radio and Television Commission waned. Media at that scale simply became too expensive a sandbox for a church denomination to play in. And Southern Baptists became embroiled in theological debate that took all their energy. My plans to work in media for my denomination fell like Humpty Dumpty off the wall.

However, I was finding great fulfillment in ministry. I became pastor of a church in North Carolina, and then in Richmond, VA. I was successful in ministry, my churches were healthy, and my young family was growing up strong. I was at an age when my network of colleagues would think of me for various positions, but nothing else seemed to fit my heart's passion and satisfy my longings as did the church.

Did my purpose change?

My career path changed, in a sense. I've always felt my purpose has been to assist, to help, to enable. Even in high school and college, I always tried to help make life easier for my friends and fellow students.

★

One of the keys to discovery of your purpose is to identify the things you enjoy. Whatever your purpose, you're not going to find it at the end of a long road of drudgery and dread. When do you feel most fulfilled? When does your spirit soar? What invigorates you?

The characteristics of who you are reveal themselves early. You are born with your personality. It can evolve, it can be modified, but it doesn't basically change. My personality in first grade that prompted teachers to give me responsibility they didn't hand to others was really no different from this five-year-old walking down the street with my father in Gaffney, South Carolina.

A street radio reporter with a microphone approached us and asked me what I wanted to be when I grew up. I said "preacher," and I was just five years old.

Lo and behold, look what I've become.

I started moving toward fulfilling my unique purpose early by being a part of what was going on wherever I was. I was the only first-grader selected to participate in the second grade talent show. In eighth grade, I was selected from the entire school to represent students and speak at the retirement of the school principal.

Getting to College

From my earliest years, I've wanted to know more about my world and have wanted to do something on behalf of the disadvantaged, the underdog. I've been friend to rich and influential people, and they have helped the causes for which I've worked along the way. But I haven't been drawn into that circle.

In college at UNC Chapel Hill, I was in the same journalism class as Karen Parker, the university's first black female student. I was one of the first people who actually welcomed her as an individual and friend, not just as "the first black female." She tells me even half a century later that I was like a big brother to her.

Our friendship was so obvious that I was even called into the Dean of Men's office and cautioned about how my reputation may suffer if I became labeled too strongly as her friend.

When the civil rights protests broke out in Chapel Hill in the fall of 1963, I along with photographer friend Jim Wallace, covered it all for the **Daily Tar Heel**. It was ugly, but we knew that history was being made and we wanted to be there.

We saw people being kicked, dragged off and hauled into paddy wagons. It was disorienting, really, but I knew that I was an eyewitness to history, and something compelled me toward the scenes that I knew people would be writing about into the next century.

Karen, reasonably, took it more personally and joined in the marches and protests, eventually being arrested.

★

Fifty years later, she, Jim and I related our involvement in the civil rights movement for a panel discussion during the 50th reunion of my Class of 1964.

Karen divulged that I had recently joked with her about our participation in the movement: "Jim took the pictures, I wrote the stories and you — you went to jail."

Finding your purpose is never a tightly-tied, blue-ribbon, finish-line, "Ta Da" kind of thing. Purpose evolves as you develop passions and strengths as a person. Whatever your ultimate purpose, you may not be ready to assume those reins now. The journey of life and your choices prepare you.

And, I dare say, your ultimate purpose will always be something that challenges you to become more.

Where I am today is not where I was 10 years ago. I'm in the same "job" but I'm not in the same place internally. I have evolved — made progress through experience — and making progress is meaningful and soul satisfying.

As my speech teacher Arthur Joseph told me many times when I resisted the voice strengthening and articulation exercises he was drumming into me, "The routine is never routine."

Finding your purpose is not about determining your vocation and climbing the professional ladder. It's about growing into and becoming who you are,

★

allowing yourself to embrace both the joy and the pain of that growing process.

Don't be bound by artificial barriers. Even the avoidance of pain is an artificial barrier. Knock down those barriers because you realize that something worthwhile, revealing and enjoyable lies just on the other side.

Inventor Thomas Edison said, "Many of life's failures are people who did not realize how close they were to success when they gave up."

My working days for many years were confined to car and office. That was my space. In a big world, that's a tiny space. I wanted to break out of the artificial barriers that such spaces created around me, so I signed up for a leadership course that included the elements of Outward Bound.

Participants are knocked out of their comfort zones. We explored things we'd never explored. We solo rafted the Nantahala River, climbed rock faces with bare hands, clung ferociously to a cable zip line skimming above the tree tops.

Yes, I was scared half to death. But I didn't die, and therefore I've pushed the boundaries of fear much further to the edges of my life than they were before. I can go further with confidence. I can risk more.

Such an exercise gets one out of one's comfort zone. When you get through it you can say, "I really did it." You experience a burst of euphoria and adrenaline that you wouldn't have if you had been satisfied with the marketing brochure and the daydream.

It is important to prove yourself to yourself. Maybe that's the best proving because ultimately you're the one you live with. When you prove to yourself that you are a man or a woman without limits, then your success is sure no matter to what purpose you ultimately apply your hand.

Seek mastery of wherever your passion points you. Seek to get better at something that matters, make progress in something meaningful to you.

My personal mantra, repeated especially before victories and following defeats, is "pure determination and the relentless pursuit of excellence."

You know from countless sports clichés born from real life moments that it is not always the most talented, smartest, prettiest, tallest, fastest, or richest competitor who wins. Like Rudy in the wonderful Notre Dame football movie, or the fictional prize fighter Rocky, it is so often the most determined person—the one who simply will not give up in the face of all odds—who ultimately wins.

You can do what you determine to do. It's your inner person who determines. You may have gifts in certain areas—you most certainly do—but it is not the gifts that will determine what you eventually accomplish. It will be the level of determination you exert to utilize those gifts.

★

Too often, we let the perceptions of others keep us from doing what we can do. Remember the 2009 "Britain's Got Talent" show contestant Susan Boyle? In that arena populated with young, hip, agile performers, she stepped out in a dowdy dress with graying, tussled hair and dared to lay her dream on the table.

Judge Simon Cowell asked her age. At 47, she was twice as old as most contestants. Then, before she put the microphone to her face to sing "The Dream" from **Les Miserables**, a judge asked her to name her own dream. Without any sense of irony or hesitation she said, "I'm trying to be a professional singer."

Cameras panning the audience recorded the snickers and face palms of embarrassed disbelief. And then she opened her mouth, and within seconds the entire audience was on its feet. Susan Boyle has gone on to fame as a professional singer and international recording artist.

Don't let anyone tell you that your dream is beyond your doing. You can do it.

In fact, that's the phrase I often use when a friend or employee is struggling at a task. "You can do this," I tell them. So often, just that word of encouragement is the only spark required to ignite their fire to burn through that task.

Develop your best traits

What characteristics can you develop that will support your determination? After all, you can be

★

determined to run a four-minute mile, but without certain attributes, it simply is not possible. You can be determined to rise from the mailroom to the CEO's corner office, but if you don't nurture certain attributes, it will not be possible.

As I've climbed from the plateau to run the high ridges, I realize I was developing three particular attributes that proved key for me: They are physical strength, emotional resilience and spiritual depth.

At age 74, I may be stronger than I've ever been. I'm not a body builder, and don't expect me to lift a car you're pinned under. But I don't dread stairs, I easily carry my own bags, and if my lawn needs a bag of lime, I can haul it out of the store myself.

As I outline in the chapter on health, I pursue a specific cardio and weightlifting routine that keeps me fit.

Emotional resilience emanates from your core. How do you respond to the slights, disappointments or tragic events in your life? Unfortunately, these are the kinds of things that test, prove, and strengthen this trait.

The very notion of "resilience" implies that you are bouncing back from something, and if you need to "bounce back," that something was a negative. You can gain emotional resilience by realizing that it's not all about you. The Universe hasn't conspired to do you dirt; God doesn't hate your football team; there is life after your divorce, and your teenager is not the

★

only one who hates her parents.

No one event "ruins your life." Your plans may be altered, your destination may suddenly require more time or money to achieve, you may be temporarily embarrassed, but cultivating emotional resilience will help you weather storms.

For me, spiritual depth is paramount. I'm not talking about giving thanks at mealtime. Spiritual depth comes from a conscious commitment to seek the heart and mind of God. "Depth" is what it implies—it's found in the deep places of the soul, not in the shallows of performance and platitudes.

Jesus spoke to it constantly, denigrating the self-righteous pseudo piety of the Pharisees in favor of the man who knew his sins made him unworthy of grace, but who recognized and was grateful for that very grace granted.

Seek God, and seek God in the deep places. Don't be satisfied to check off worship attendance or toss $20 in the offering plate and call that spiritual depth. Go to the scary places where revelation may sear your soul. Strip it bare until you crawl like a sun-bleached skeleton before God, ultimately to rise with a greater, fuller knowledge of who you are in relation to the Creator.

Any investigation of discovering purpose must answer the question, "Am I making a contribution?" and its corollary, "Does my contribution matter?"

From my youngest years, I've wanted to lessen

★

the suffering of children. I find myself now in
a position to do just that. I'm fulfilled in that. Does my
contribution matter? I'm absolutely convinced it does,
and I spend much of every week working to convince
others that their support of this work matters—not
just to me, but to the children and families we serve.

In this arena—and this has been a long time
coming—I've finally come to embrace the reality that
I matter. I, Michael Clitus Blackwell, matter. This is
not to say I'm an egomaniac, or that the Baptist Children's Homes could not be led effectively by another.

I'm saying that nothing I've done would
have been done in precisely the same way if another
person was doing it. I'm saying that I've found my
Purpose—helping hurting children. . .healing broken
families.

It is also to say that for the first time, I have
a sense that who I am matters to others. Through staff
members and friends, word gets back to me that those
little things I've done mean a great deal more to the
people who receive them than I ever would have
expected.

It's humbling to know that it means a lot to
people to get a call or a visit from me. Although I'll
always (proudly) be the boy from the mill village,
I've recently begun to embrace the realization of who
I am to others because of the children we serve.

They know I'm busy, and that because of my
work, I have some influence among those whom

★

others feel are important. I'm usually the one on the stage or the pulpit. In our culture, these things work to establish a distance between the stage personality and the audience.

I bridge that gap at every opportunity as a natural consequence of my personality. People want to be heard, and too few of us take the time to listen.

If someone feels that I lend them my ears and stop my forward motion to listen, to really understand, and to hear what they're saying, that elevates their self-perception. To care is part of my purpose.

They will stand straighter with head high and shoulders back.

When they ask a follow-up question and I let them talk, they perceive I can be trusted, and that's part of my purpose.

I am present when I talk with anyone. I am an eye-contact person now, way more than I used to be. I used to look at someone's mouth when I talked to them. Now I look them in the eyes. I connect and I listen.

This trait might seem so natural that you wonder why I'm mentioning it. But, I'm telling you, I'm in a small minority. People don't tend to listen to others — they just perch in the conversation, waiting to leap in to make their own statement. People will beat a path to the door of someone who listens.

One day I reached for the phone and called Mr. R.K. Hancock, the influential school principal of my youth. I simply told him how much he meant to me, how his confidence in me boosted and nurtured my confidence in myself.

We spent an hour on the phone, sobbing much of the time. Our tears washed away the years. I wished I hadn't gone so long without telling him what he meant to me. That experience prompted me to make many other calls.

On the most recent Mother's Day, I called seven mothers (all widows), including a woman whose son is on my board of trustees. At the next board meeting, he came in extolling how his mother couldn't get over the fact that I'd called her to wish her well on Mother's Day.

My call simply affirmed each of them. I'm not saying that a call on their special Hallmark Card Day doesn't mean anything to fathers, but it simply means more to a woman. Call your mother regularly and never forget her on Mother's Day.

A big part of why I felt good after making those calls is because I did not anticipate how good it would make them feel. But, that's a part of finding and living my purpose: discovering how I feel about who I am.

Today, I'm newly-confident, sure-footed and grazing the high ground. That doesn't mean I've escaped every moment of self-doubt and insecurity. One of my generation's finest actresses, Meryl Streep, says self-doubt has sometimes crippled her to the

★

point of being unable to get out of bed. I've sometimes not wanted to get out of bed, but it's never been
because of self-doubt.

Affirmation

Affirmation is a great way to ease the self-doubt
in others. It's easy to do. Learn a little something
about a person. Call them by their name as you
converse. There's nothing sweeter to a person than
the sound of that person's name.

Don't be phony. Find something specific
and mean it. Compliment a smile that "lights up
the room." Appreciate a "nice voice." Comment
positively—like my daughter once did on the glorious
head of white hair on an elderly gentleman in
a restaurant.

We need affirmation. The human spirit needs it.

When someone says they enjoyed spending
time with me, I feel affirmed. It helps me accept that
as a part of my purpose.

I confess that I need affirmation every bit as
much as the next guy. When I've prepared hard to
master an event, I like to hear from participants that it
was meaningful for them. When I take extra care with
my appearance, I like my wife to notice—and tell me.
I like to receive a pat on the back from my board.

Without the occasional positive stroke, it's hard
to keep your footing on the ridge, and you may just
fall into the abyss.

What happens if the affirmation or recognition

★

doesn't come? That means you must be self-sufficient and sure of your course. It's harder without the pat on the back that says you're doing well, but don't be deterred.

I appreciate the wisdom of the **Star Wars** character Yoda. When he encouraged Luke Skywalker to use The Force and raise his star fighter from beneath the swamp where it had crashed, Luke said, "I'll give it a try."

"Do or do not," Yoda said. "There is no try."

I understand the concept of "trying." You give it your best shot and hope you accomplish the goal. If you do, great. If you don't, keep at it. But "I'll give it a try" is not the refrain of confidence, or of mastery.

To demonstrate "try" at a motivational seminar, I had Sam, my Senior VP, "try" to catch a ball I tossed to him. He caught it.

"No, no," I said. "Try to catch the ball."

He couldn't try to catch it. He either caught it, or he didn't.

"Casual" has become the dress code of choice for virtually all business interactions today. In the denominational structure of the agency I lead, I must make an annual presentation to appeal for budget funds. The organizational leader of that committee meeting wrote to tell me that it is an informal event and to dress casually.

While I appreciated the heads-up, I didn't follow the guideline; I wore a tie and blazer. It's not my outfit that will get my request approved, but my personal presentation set me apart from others. If committee members remembered nothing of what I said, they remembered that I treated them with professional respect and that I treated myself as someone with a purpose and passion for my plea.

My friend in grade school graduated at the top of his class. He was always studious. Good grades were their own reward for him, and he wasn't involved in anything at school but academics. He went to college at NC State, had a nice job, made a good living, had some health issues. He moved steadily through his days but he never soared as everyone expected.

Then he retired. I once asked him what he does during his retirement.

"I don't do anything," he said. And he meant just that. He never leaves the house, doesn't go anywhere, or see anybody, or engage with people or organizations or causes. This is a good friend. We went trick-or-treating together as children. And he always edged me out in school competitions.

But, he never reached his potential. He settled into a level of comfort on the prairie that sated any desire he might have had to run the ridges.

Your purpose is to discover your potential and then to go for it. Everybody is born with potential.

At the Children's Homes, we are blessed by some of our developmental disabilities ministry residents who have Down Syndrome. When we have a big presentation, they will stand before a convention center full of people and sing, unshackled by expectation. They feel affirmed by the warm smiles and applause that comes back to them.

They have potential. They have purpose. God gives every person the capacity to find a life purpose to which they can devote their passion. Too many lose sight of that, and their dreams slog down around their ankles until they can barely walk.

I feel sorry for those souls, and I can't pass anybody panhandling without giving them money. I look them in the eye, recognize their humanity — and for a fleeting second — pass them hope and a connection. That's a part of my purpose.

No matter how long a person lives, your time on this stage is brief. We make the most of our moment or two, and then we're gone. If we're lucky we'll have kids and grandchildren who will remember who we are.

The work I do draws accolades. Because I'm the leader, I get more credit than I deserve for our good work. If I die when I'm in office, there'll be a large funeral for me.

I'm realistic enough to know that if I die a year after I leave office, the Ladies Circle at church won't have to make more than two dozen sandwiches to serve all who come.

Don't read any of that as being pessimistic.

★

No one running the ridge is pessimistic. I'm just committed not to go to my grave with my music still inside me.

I want to play my song before the music dies.

Many people find their song after retirement, so you can't equate vocation with purpose. Can you think of someone who blossomed and flourished after he or she retired from their career task?

Crafting a personal mission statement was popular and almost mandatory for a season in a wave of "success" books. It's fallen off the mantra list but it still may be a good idea for you.

What do you think about when you get up in the morning? What's on your mind when you slip beneath the covers at night? My ever-present thought is about what I've done — or failed to do — to make life better for children that day.

Those things that occupy your mind at your first and last thoughts of the day reflect your passion. In pursuing yours, think of Julian Treasure's TED Talk (TED is a nonpartisan nonprofit devoted to spreading ideas, usually in the form of short powerful talks) acronym HAIL to provide a four-cornered, life-centering mantra: Honesty, Authenticity, Integrity, Love. Recognizing, reaching and living those qualities is a part of your purpose, no matter your vocation.

Live your own truth: You cannot be squeezed, molded, crammed, clipped or coerced into anyone else's expectations and still discover your purpose.

★

I'll repeat this sentiment, because it is so important and so common: Success is nothing but the accumulated wisdom from a bunch of failures.

You're going to fail. That doesn't mean for a minute that you're a failure. Claim the rocks of failure as the steppingstones on which to build your success.

Don't surrender the dream. If it's viable, and it's got hold of you like a bulldog, don't let it go.

I wanted to go to the University of North Carolina, and when my path seemed blocked, I clung to the dream. The connections I made in Chapel Hill set my early course.

When I was in high school, I knew beyond a shadow of doubt that I was going to win the Jefferson Standard college scholarship, which would pay for my college education. Jefferson owned WBT and WBTV; I was already in radio and planned to major in radio, television and motion pictures.

I didn't get it. And my friend who did get it was not involved in media and didn't intend to pursue media as a career. I was crushed and thought, "There goes my free ride."

I had to back up and reevaluate my plans. Could I still go to Carolina? My hopes for particular funding had not developed. But that was my dream, and I found another way for it to work—holding down three part-time jobs.

Early in your pursuit of purpose, you will

★

28

extend your antennae in many directions and listen to lots of advice. You'll have more options on your plate and more possibilities than you can imagine, and you may want to do it all.

Of course, if everything is a priority, then nothing is a priority. Keep your goals list to no more than three. They may change, but when you start your day, or your month or your year and plot where you would like to be at the end of that time segment, you should have no more than three goals on the graph.

"No" is an option. People-pleasers tend to say "yes" to anything they're asked to do. That will not keep you at your peak productivity. Do fewer things and do them well.

Do the important things first, and do them now.

In my current position, both professionally and in life, I focus on the things that only I can do. If someone else can do it, I let them. Or I ask them to. I concentrate on doing the things that I, alone, am gifted and tasked to do, or that I am responsible for by position.

Others can order the office supplies. Others can keep the fleet records, and do the books, and plan some meetings, and settle some disputes. But board issues, strategic planning, major donor cultivation and crises fall into my lap. They are issues for the CEO.

If I had 20 people reporting directly to me,

★

I'd have 20 areas to claim my attention and disperse my effectiveness. I now have only three direct reports, and I concentrate on big-picture tableaus. That helps me stay nimble on the ridge in a condition I never could maintain if I were carrying the weight of 20 different saddlebags.

I find that I can do anything once I stop trying to do everything.

ACHIEVEMENT

No. 2

Creating something
that outlasts you

★

CHAPTER 2

Making a World of Difference

In 1983, trustees of the Baptist Children's
Homes of North Carolina elected me president of
the organization that served more than 2,000 children
each year through a 13-facility network that stretched
across the state. BCH is one of the oldest and largest
child-caring institutions in the Southeast.

BCH was two years from celebrating its
centennial. Its previous president had served 25 years
and before that one of its chief executives had been
encouraged to run for governor of North Carolina.
He declined in favor of the "more important" work
of serving children.

The scope of the office and its status in the
state was larger than I knew when I said "yes" to
the committee that put my name forward for election.

On the day they affirmed me as president,
I achieved a position for which I had not yearned,
and had not yet earned. I was a pastor, albeit with

★

an unusual path to the pulpit.

The title on my business card said "President."
That was my position, my responsibility, my pay
grade. But I held that title only because 36 strangers
who trusted their committee cast their vote for me.

Two years later, at the 1985 meeting of North
Carolina Baptists in Charlotte, I asked Jim Johnson,
one of our resident childcare workers, to tell this con-
gress of supportive churches just what it was like to
live in a cottage with 12 children, charged with their
nurture, care and feeding; on call around the clock;
to be disciplinarian, dad and devoted counselor.

Jim was one of the dearest and sincerest men
I've ever known, and I was proud to see him rise and
walk to the microphone to address the crowd of 2,500.

Because his heart is like butter, it melted
under the harsh stage lights. Jim started sobbing as
he told the stories of young people he and his wife,
Vivian, had known and helped as cottage parents.
Jim couldn't finish, and while the crowd was entirely
supportive, eventually it grew awkward.

I walked across the stage and put my arm
around this man who epitomized every good thing
about working with children. We shared a brief
moment with the crowd and I walked with Jim
to the side of the stage and the rest of the program
continued.

Later, BCH trustee Faye Broyhill told me it
was that moment when I became president of Baptist

★

Children's Homes. I had achieved the position, which until then had been just a title.

Men and women are driven to achieve, to bring to a successful end a task once started.

We tend to consider achievement in terms of greatness, i.e. showing "bigness." If we haven't had our name in lights, or been recognized with 15 minutes of fame, or even been the subject of a trending Twitter hashtag, we think we will go to our graves without ever having achieved anything.

Here is good news for you: There is no more room on Mount Rushmore, so let's redefine achievement.

I define achievement as creating something that's going to outlast you.

The thing about achievement is there are measuring sticks involved. You don't achieve something unless you can measure that position against a lower plateau.

Money may be a good measure, but for simplicity let me ask: If you were born a millionaire and died a millionaire, what did you achieve? You leave with only what you had when you came.

At one time, I thought about the people who go to work from 9 to 5, punch the clock and go home. Their goal is to be able to keep doing that until they can retire. Then I realized that just their ability to be faithful, dedicated, and consistent in that task in an economy constantly in flux is an achievement.

★

They've achieved because they've fed their family. They've kept a roof over their heads, educated their children, showed up at parent-teacher meetings. They may not register "achievement" in the creative process, but the truth is if they didn't assemble the widgets correctly, the company doesn't achieve and the workers lose their livelihood, which enabled all the achievements above.

In many cases, they're happy doing what they do day by day. For them, that's achievement.

Don, our talented maintenance director, succeeds in his role. I couldn't be the maintenance person. Our staff would all be walking around in the dark if I had to change the light bulbs.

Don keeps our workplace and our cottages functioning. You know how aggravated you can get when the window sticks, gutters are clogged, the toilet is jammed, or the driveway is breaking up.

All talented people who take care of those tasks keep us from grinding to a halt. That maintenance role is as important and as much a success as any other. As the Bill Staines song says, "All God's creatures got a place in the choir."

Maybe the world doesn't acknowledge the important things you do, but what you do makes a world of difference. Are you a good parent? Are you a good son or daughter to an aging and discouraged parent? Are you a good neighbor, with whom neighborhood kids feel safe and know they can get

★

a cookie or a smile of approval when they are feeling sad or lonely?

A lot of people work hard to be successful grandparents. It's a different chance, a second chance to pour yourself into grandchildren when career and ambition might have robbed your children of having more of you.

You may derive your sense of achievement from something as self-satisfying as finishing a certain book, earning a degree as an adult, or any other goal you set.

It's OK to find something that enables you to say, "I've achieved." It may be a weight loss, or a health goal. You've given up chemical-laced, sugar-laden soft drinks. You regularly eat a carrot instead of a candy bar, and that eating habit has become a part of your conscious healthful diet.

Claim it: Real achievement comes from a challenge. Maybe you've taught first-graders in Sunday School for 20 years. Now you're attending their weddings. Wow. What an achievement!

Achieving

So, you want to make a mark. You want to flee this mortal coil with something that outlasts the fleeting breath of your life. How do you do it?

As I've told countless young people who wonder what they should do with their lives, "Discover your passion." What is it that turns you on, makes your heart soar, gets you excited, and makes you

★

jump out of bed in the morning? What do you enjoy and wish you could do more? Where do you get a sense of achievement?

Do you know your strengths? Do you know your weaknesses? Are you good at a task because you love it, or do you love it because you're good at it? It doesn't matter! If something gives you joy, pursue it.

Find a mentor who is thriving in an area in which you have an interest. You'd be surprised to learn how many professionals and expert tradesmen are willing to help a sincere, eager person who wants to learn from their experience. Enthusiasm counts because there are many people today who are blasé about life and opportunity.

Your mentor should be strong, not threatened by your energy and passion. In my first church staff position, my ambition, excitement and personality could have overwhelmed the pastor, but he was not threatened and gave me room to operate.

No matter what you do, give it all you have. If you are employed beneath your education, work that job like it's the fulfillment of your every employment fantasy. If you treat it as beneath you, your conduct in the job will reflect poorly to anyone who may be considering you for a better job.

Stick it out. Time matters. Experts say recent college graduates entering the job market today will have an average of 26 careers before they retire. That's impossible! They may have 26 jobs, but no one who spends only two years at a job and moves on has created a career there.

"Time in grade" is the military term when being considered for advancement. I could have advanced pretty quickly in my early careers, but I was still sorting things out before responding to the call to ministry. I worked for the Durham *Morning Herald* and was pegged to move up, but after four months I moved to Charlotte to pursue my passion for radio.

My greater passion for ministry overtook that love, and I later moved toward Raleigh where I worked in television to support my family while I studied at seminary. My track isn't typical, but I know from experience that my earlier observations are true. Sticking through a rough patch, taking on a tough assignment, showing loyalty to the company goals when they don't conflict with your own moral center is important to advancing.

Achievement in life is about lots more than your career. But we're talking about career here, so learn to study the company culture. You advance in your company culture by getting along with your supervisor. Your supervisor will have charge of your destiny within the company and many times, outside the company.

He or she will help you progress or keep you from progressing. He or she can fire you, promote you, marginalize you, undercut you, turn away inquiries about you as a potential employee with

★

another company, or take a personal interest in your career and be proud when you do well.

Develop your skills and keep learning new skills. Work hard, take advantage of cross-training opportunities. Get in there and do what you're asked, and then do more. Stay a little later. Come a little early. Find a way to walk by the boss's office when you're there putting in extra time. Odds are, he or she will be there too and will notice that you're sharing his/her work ethic.

We had an intern once who was late every day. One day he came into his supervisor's office, frustrated. He said, "I don't understand it. I leave home at the same time every day, but I'm always 15 minutes late."

When I was doing my weight-loss process, I wanted shortcuts: I wanted to lose 10 pounds overnight and keep eating Krispy Kreme doughnuts while I watched the weight melt away.

I'm more process-oriented now than goal-oriented. When you set a goal, concentrate on your behaviors and then trust the process. You're after progress, not perfection.

Without giving you an easy out, I want to remind you that you're not a failure if you don't meet your goal. You're a failure if you don't have a goal. Keep your eye on the prize. Don't be satisfied with mediocrity.

The diabolical twin to achievement is recogni-

★

tion. What happens when you feel you've achieved something that few — if any — others have and it happens anonymously? There are no hands clapping, no banner raised, and no headline in tomorrow's newspaper.

I've been recognized and applauded in many ways through my decades as president of Baptist Children's Homes of North Carolina. My board has recognized my service, a biography was written about me. I'm usually the featured speaker when I attend special events, and the applause and positive comments afterward are gratifying. I confess right here: I love it.

I love the energy that flows between the crowd and me. Any performer will tell you that the audience is a life source. Their positive response to your words is unadulterated energy flowing from their tank into your engine.

But, what happens when the recognition doesn't come? What happens when you've done your best, felt like you made a mark, improved the product or the process and the world just yawns? Your boss is oblivious, your spouse doesn't get it, and the dog doesn't even wag its tail?

It doesn't feel good. But rather than lamenting what you're not getting, let it be a lesson for ridge running. Recognition counts and you will do well to find opportunities to recognize others — even if you're not getting any positive recognition yourself.

★

People thrive from a pat on the back, an attaboy, a personal note, a positive comment about them from you in front of their peers. Some studies indicate that being positively recognized and obviously appreciated by their bosses means more to most people than a pay increase. When you're living your passion, outside recognition is not as important. Your joy and deep satisfaction emanate outward from within.

It's taken me a while to learn this. It just didn't dawn on me that as "the president," and now as "Dr. Blackwell," or even as "Big Daddy," a positive word from me matters. People respond like a cat arching its back to get a scratch.

It matters that I notice. Our employees get a positive stroke from their supervisor, but getting it from the president is an entirely different thing. Positive strokes from me must be sincere, and I can do that easily because I sincerely do appreciate our people. But how do I show it?

I make phone calls. I call out names during public events. I send a note with a scripture and encouraging word. I give a responsibility to someone who might have thought she's not up to it. Suddenly, being asked by me to do it, being recognized by me as capable of doing it, that person rises to the expectation and astounds even herself.

My administrative staff has a Monday morning meeting at which we catch up with each other and hear a devotional word. Some of us are ministers.

★

Much to her surprise, I asked my office manager to lead a devotional in the future for a much larger venue.

That request didn't put her on the spot or embarrass her. Instead, it motivated her because the president saw her as capable.

At a large regional meeting, one of our female residents sang. It was lovely, but the girl felt that her performance was horrible. She apologized to me in tears and said it was the worst job she'd ever done.

I said, "Stop it right there. Repeat after me, 'I did a good job.' She said, "I did a good job," and I ask her to repeat it: "I did a good job. I was a blessing to these people."

While she thought she had to apologize, I asked, "Did you hear the ovation you got? They couldn't stop applauding."

"You did good," I told her, and asked her to repeat it yet again. "I did good," she said, and she finally believed it. I don't mess around with negative anymore.

Some folks may think (or assume) that ridge runners don't need any reassurances. Actually, we all enjoy hearing the occasional compliment. Always have the integrity of sincerity when offering praise or compliments to anyone.

A good compliment lasts all month. People crave that stuff. We want to be validated and recognized. We want to feel that what we do matters and

★

know that somebody noticed it.

Listen. Get to know something about the person. Maintain eye contact. Be aware. Know when to affirm and be ready to offer a kind word.

A young woman at the YMCA where I work out was obviously pregnant, which is an easy enough starting point for conversation. I learned the baby was due close to the birth dates of my son and my father. I joked that if it was born on either day, I'd have a nice surprise for her.

She missed those dates, but when her little girl was born, I asked to see pictures and showed genuine interest. What new mom doesn't light up when someone shows interest in her child?

That's what it's about. It's just a natural thing and no trouble at all. Just get out of yourself and into others.

Note the way people's eyes and faces glow when you notice them. People want to be noticed. It would be the very rare, ultra-introverted person who truly wants to go through a day unnoticed. I believe that. If they give me a chance and look at me, I'll notice them. I'm not going to knock anyone down, but with a smile and a returned gaze, I'll build them up.

To bless a child is a blessing. And I'm able to do that now because of the confidence I have earned from a life of successfully seeing tasks through to completion—achieving. I can say from the ridge, "Come on up, the view is good from here."

★

At this point you exude an attitude of generosity. Not only can you afford to be generous because you've reached the peak, but you realize you've much to give because much has been given to you.

When you are in ascendency, people are watching. You never know what that might mean, except when the time comes that someone will have to make a judgment about you, it's likely that person will remember your generosity.

Poet, novelist and professor Maya Angelou said people remember you not for what you say, but for how you make them feel.

The leader of our service to developmentally disabled adults wrote me a heart-wrenching note; she was distraught because she was going to have to discharge a resident with bipolar illness. We could not accommodate the level of the resident's psychological dysfunction.

I responded, noting my appreciation for her service to our residents and empathizing with the decision that was causing her stress. She wrote back, saying, "Please know your kind words have lifted me today. It meant so much hearing *you* say that."

The encouragement could have come from anyone. But she said that it meant a lot, "especially coming from you."

To be idle is selfish. Idleness indicates that your self is your main concern. When you're moving, you're growing and helping other people grow.

★

The Bible talks about talents we are given, and we are charged with investing and developing those talents for the benefit of the Master. Are you using the gifts and talents made available to you? Are you satisfied with where you are and what you've achieved?

It's not selfish to want more when you truly understand what "more" is and why you want it. Do you want more for selfish reasons, or to help other people; to advance your career at the expense of others, or to position yourself to be a positive factor for others?

When you achieve more — more money, more experience, more knowledge, more time, more fame — that means you need to share more. That's one reason I'm writing this book.

I want to share some elements essential for thriving at the peak. Generosity is one of those elements. It's when we share that we build a community that will cooperate to overcome hard times.

As a ridge runner, I must ask, "Is there more for me?"

- I'm at the peak, but I'm not satisfied. What's that cloud over there? Is that cloud hiding yet another peak for me to climb?
- I'm at the point where I can look out over the vast plains below and say this has gone well so far, but I'm still dreaming. I want to study and manage our assets to the maximum benefit for our organization and the children we serve.

★

- I want to develop a plan that enables men and women who have been supporters for years to stay involved with us, no matter to which church they belong.
- I don't want to become complacent. If I can't inspire and dazzle anymore, that's my signal that it's time to be done here. The calendar is not dictating that for me. The bright and shining dream dictates that for me.

My mind doesn't let me stop when I've set and achieved goals; it simply establishes new goals. We're still thinking, planning, hoping, and moving forward.

I didn't create Baptist Children's Homes, and it certainly will outlast me, but it will bear my DNA for a generation because I've been able to shape it and redefine it.

In fact, I consider my greatest achievement that after 33 years of my presidency, the Baptist Children's Homes—and all its varied ministries—is stronger and more viable now than ever. The fact that we are widely known as cultivating a culture of excellence within a strong Christian framework is of unspeakable value.

Baptist Children's Homes wasn't founded by me, but I feel like I've had the honor of being allowed to lead and participate in creating something here. When we did our first capital campaign, our consultant told us "the institution is the lengthened shadow of the president."

★

I didn't buy that in 1992 but I buy it now.

I was a person when I came into this position. But as my mentor Bill Friday once reminded me, "You are a personage now, Mickey."

With that image comes great responsibility and a requirement for great integrity and humility. My reputation and that of this institution are inextricably linked. It's taken me a lifetime to establish whatever reputation I have, and it's taken Baptist Children's Homes 131 years to establish its current reputation.

Both can be destroyed in a few seconds.

Protect your reputation: It is your integrity, and it's far easier to keep it than it is to repair it.

There is no single event or position that is a universal measure of achievement. Your career is one thing, but other areas of your life will benefit from the same process I've suggested above. Set goals in areas of life beyond your job.

Do you want to be a better spouse? What would that entail? Listening more? Learning your spouse's love language and speaking it?

Do you want to run a marathon? Start by getting off the couch and walking around the block. Every journey has a first step and every goal is achievable with commitment to a plan and a process.

You'll know you've achieved something when you can reach and embrace the goal that you set. The satisfaction you enjoy will affirm that achieving that goal was worth all the work.

★

RELATIONSHIPS

No. 3

Nurture the ones
who make life work

★

CHAPTER 3

Blessing the Tie that Binds

I didn't know the caller that well when I answered the phone in my office almost three decades ago. A man I knew only as an alumnus of the residential children's homes system I've led since 1983 was on the line. We had met briefly at an alumni function, and he lived locally.

He seemed morose, discouraged, at loose ends and disconnected from a world that never seemed to be a welcoming place for kids who grew up knowing their biological family did not, could not, would not care for them. He talked. I listened. I encouraged.

By the end of the conversation, it seemed the dark cloud hovering over him was breaking up a bit. He could see some narrow shafts of light streaming into his life.

I hung up, grateful for the chance to speak some hope into a life, and went back to my task at hand.

Over the next several decades, he and I spoke

briefly on several occasions, such as at alumni reunions or around town. He was not always a fan of the changes I had to implement at the Home that he and his classmates considered sacred, inviolable and unchangeable. But we were always civil and worked through any disagreements.

Then one day, I received a letter in which he brought up our telephone conversation from 30 years earlier. I hadn't thought much about it; he had seemed to be doing well, and our relationship was merely cordial.

He recalled our long-ago conversation in his letter and had written to thank me.

"I was down and depressed," he said. "I don't even know why I called you instead of someone else, but I did. And you about saved my life that day."

To me, that's an example of what relationships are about: The interaction and intentional nurturing of other human beings whose paths have magically, logically, accidentally, and magnificently crossed yours.

When you've climbed to the peak and have surveyed the vast horizon spread at your feet, what is the one element in your recipe for satisfaction from this point forward?

If you've arrived alone — with no family behind you, no colleagues genuinely pleased with your achievements, no peers you brought with you — your arrival will ring hollow and unsatisfying. We are

★

made for relationships, and the simple truth is that you did not arrive without nurturing relationships.

The questions we might ask are:

- How have you treated those relationships that helped you?
- How do you develop relationships that will be mutually supportive?
- How do you maintain relationships that will be satisfying for the rest of your journey?

Relationships are so important that studies show the person who is adept around the water cooler is more likely to be promoted than a co-worker with a similar skill level who merely grinds out the work every day. If you are production-oriented, God bless you. Every manager loves a stable full of people just like you.

However, if you are interested in moving forward with your career, you may want to lift your head from the computer or the telephone or the assembly line sometimes and pay attention to the people around you. Do you know their names? Get to know them by name. Ask them about their interests? Has someone been away for a while? Who likes the Atlanta Braves? Who's a Carolina Panthers fan?

You may not even like sports, but many others do. It pays to cultivate an awareness so you can participate in the Monday conversations that inevitably start with, "How 'bout them Bears?" or whatever the local team is.

★

I know a number of people who absolutely have the professional skills, education, grasp of task and experience to be much further along in life and career than they are. But they are people who are so production-oriented, they neglected to establish peer relationships.

People are becoming more isolated from each other. Isolation leads to all kinds of problems, including obesity, depression and anxiety. Houses of worship are great places to find and establish relationships with like-minded people — no matter what "minded" you are because worship settings themselves are so varied.

If you think you are so unusual that you can't find anyone else like you with whom to establish relationships, think about this: Those who attend a particular house of worship are similar-minded about the things that matter most — their relationship to God and to each other. Within that context, you'll find a wide variety of opinion on all the other categories of life: politics, sports, schools, national minimum wage, and whether the pandas in the National Zoo are cute.

Isolation is not good. Relationships are good.

Which relationships in your life matter most to you? Who are the people whose absence would most negatively affect your life, whom you would miss most? Are you nurturing those relationships? Are you eating lunch alone every day so you can get right back to work? Do you take a lap around the office, "managing by walking around," so people know you're approachable?

How about a personality check? Are you always buttoned up? Do you allow anyone at the office to see you as anything beyond an office drone? If your job is delivering packages, do you linger to talk when you get back to the shop, or even go for pizza with a co-worker?

It may be the case that you work with a crew with whom you want no further contact after work or in anything other than work. Still, nurture relationships within that working environment because these are the people who, first of all, will be the most help to you in your own job, and secondly, they are the people whose recommendations will be a key to your next job.

Beyond professional networks we tend to equate relationships with "friends." How many good friends do you need for a happy life? Most people say you are fortunate indeed to have as many deep, true, trusted friendships as you have fingers on one hand. I don't have that many.

There are many people I consider to be friends. There are many people I can call upon for advice and counsel, to help in a project, to contribute to a need. I'm sure there are many who will try to correct my faults by talking to others. But is there one who cares for me deeply enough that he will help me correct my faults by speaking about them directly to me?

★

It's possible to outgrow a relationship, and even a friendship of 20 years is not worth keeping on life support. If you have to work too hard at it, and it's one-way, the most merciful act may be to let it die and begin your grief process.

The goal here is not to tell you how to end relationships. The goal is to help you identify and nurture relationships.

The very term "relationship" indicates something built over time. You don't forge a relationship with someone in the afternoon that you met for the first time at the coffee shop in the morning. One example of this is the annual homecoming we have for alumni of the Baptist Children's Homes of North Carolina.

Alumni from the 1940s, 50s and 60s attend these events faithfully every year. They had typically lived at the Children's Homes for 8-10 years and had grown up under conditions that today would be deemed harsh. A single cottage matron might have had as many as 40 children in her charge, so she ruled with an iron fist.

Children worked the farm, and the laundry and the kitchen. They were disciplined harshly—even severely by some recollections. But they were in it together and they grew up as family and still today consider themselves as brothers and sisters.

Alumni whom we served in more recent decades typically come to us not as victims of

★

a parental death and poverty but as victims of abuse and neglect. We work with them and their families to try to resolve the issues that tear the family apart. Most often the children eventually are restored to a healthier family.

Consequently, their relationship with the Children's Homes and with each other is not nearly as deep as that of alumni of a previous generation. It's the difference between plants that grew quickly in a greenhouse and those that grew slowly over time in the deep loam of fertile fields.

Relationships may ebb and flow over time, too. For a long time, one particular alumnus from the 1940s did not approve of the way I did things as BCH president. He clung to the way things were, even though in his own profession he understood that change was inevitable and desirable. At the orphanage he grew up in and loved, the memories were etched in stone, and were such a sacred part of him that he felt no future changes should erode them.

But in the past few years, this man has warmed to me in a way I never would have anticipated. When our agency was facing threats internal and external, from issues both large and small, he told me, "I don't know what we would have done without you." Some relationships you give up on, some you don't.

Actions to develop relationships

Be vulnerable. This may be the most difficult action because you open yourself to being hurt,

★

embarrassed, rejected, and even ridiculed. But you also open yourself to transparency, intimacy, friendship, and the possibility of being of like-mind and spirit with another.

Be real. Living at the peak, I no longer feel the need to build and protect a veneer that establishes a version of myself that I think I must project. Real is better. Real is easier.

If someone loves a veneer version of you, you'll find it's too much work to keep up that image, and you'll never achieve the level of transparency that genuine relationships require. You'll wear yourself out and still be lonely.

Some years ago, I was outside with Pepper, the family dog, and simply bent over to pet him. Something snapped in my back and I fell to earth with a thud. I was in such pain that I could not rise to walk back to the house—I literally had to crawl.

The reaction of friends and neighbors to this event surprised me. They were beyond sympathetic and, for some, my incident was almost a revelation that "he's human, too."

In most public situations I attend, I am the speaker. That automatically puts a little distance between me and the crowd, but I've learned to seek conversations with them now, both before and after my address. I get as much satisfaction from several one-on-one, self-revealing, give-and-take conversations as I do from addressing the crowd.

★

Vulnerability is vital to building relationships. I trust that my transparency in these pages is at least beginning to build my relationship with you.

There are many types of relationships. Here are a few examples of different ones:

I am committed to an annual visit to Structure House in Durham. It is a wellness facility and program where I spend time re-centering my diet and exercise regimen. Everyone around me is there for similar reasons.

My apartment neighbor during a recent visit struggles with spinal bifida. Getting around was very difficult for her, so I just became her daddy substitute for a week. Sometimes it tore me up to see her struggle to achieve the simplest things. I would retrieve her phone and fetch her some bananas when she was not feeling well.

I befriended a gay dancer who wasn't making friends easily. We worked out together one day. I'm beyond labels and stereotypes now, and my new freedom is less exhilarating than it is simply satisfying.

Think of how much less work it is to be yourself — to be transparent and vulnerable — than it is to build and maintain the veneers of image.

A group with whom you can be vulnerable is invaluable!

I'm part of a group of ministers that has met together two days a year for 40 years. Everything is off the record. We discuss our profession, our churches, national and world politics, frustrations and joys. We do it without judgment and without fear that our vulnerability will be used against us down the road.

It is extremely important to find someone who can be a mentor to you, a trusted associate who may be older and has some experience, who can coach you without your taking offense. Such a person can encourage you and support you in your commitment to follow through on your challenges.

A mutual friend recently was talking with a young pastor new to my town. The pastor asked our friend if he thought I might have time to mentor him.

"Of course," our friend said. "Ask him."

As bright and well trained as this young pastor is, he is not experienced enough to recognize the land mines of ministry. I have a minesweeper well tested and worn.

There is chemistry and affinity involved in finding your mentor of choice. Is there someone you want to be like? Do you see your potential mentor show up at the same meetings, or sporting events, or church? What elements or characteristics or leadership traits does that person exhibit that you would emulate?

The first time I heard a sermon by Randall Lolley, former president of Southeastern Seminary, I knew I wanted to talk to him, to learn more from him, to see if some of his style could rub off on me. He could preach the Scripture, but he did it in a way

★

that was relational and funny. He made points powerfully with humor, and I tried to soak up as much Randall as I could.

I consider the late William Friday, president of the University of North Carolina system for 30 years, as my life coach. But I say that with a caveat. Probably half of North Carolinians who ever knew this public sage would consider him a mentor in that they learned so much about life and people from him.

My relationship with him started when I was just a freshman in college. With him, I could get more inspiration and illumination in 30 minutes than I could from 10 books. Truth be told, Bill Friday was more like a hero to me than a mentor. You don't find many people who can clarify a problem or question that took you years to formulate.

I recently called Jack Gale, a radio legend I worked with when I was barely a professional. He has a golden voice and still does radio commercials at age 90. Because it's a relationship that has endured a half-century, it's important for me to continue to call him.

When he picks up the phone, I'm transported on a zipline through time. To him I'm still "Sweet C. Michael Blackwell" (my radio name), and when he asks how I'm doing, my long-scripted, now natural, response is, "I'm sweeter than ever."

Relationships require nurturing. But that's a fun part.

★

I've taken leadership courses and opened myself to staff in 360 degree evaluations. Of course, none of that has any meaning unless you evaluate the feedback without getting upset (taking it personally) and follow through for self-improvement.

Do you have a confidant? You don't need many. If you're married, I hope your spouse fulfills that role.

Your marriage is always—and must be—your primary relationship. It requires and merits attention, nurture and investment. Remember that your spouse is not your extension. He or she is an individual and needs space to pursue individual interests. Don't require that you do everything together, because when you have some separate interests, you bring back to your relationship a broader arena to share.

Don't let this marital relationship go stale. Interject surprise and novelty to keep it fresh. You neglect this at your own peril. Two people who have shared years together can continue to get along under the same roof even in the midst of benign neglect. But for your relationship to stay stimulating, invigorating, and mutually beneficial, it always must be more than toleration.

We enter marriage thinking we are living on the same plane as our new mate because we share the same values and common interests that drew us together. Then we discover over time that we really are different people. At first, we might think that's a bad thing, but if we continue to communicate, we

★

learn that different is a very good thing.

Do you know your spouse's love language? A common mistake, especially for men, is to believe that the things that make us feel good, both physically and emotionally, are the same things that make our wives feel good. So, if we like to be touched in a certain way, that's the way we touch. If we like to be silly, we assume our wives like to be silly — or at least she appreciates our silliness.

If our love language is physical intimacy, that's the language we speak when we want to show love. It's a rude awakening to learn that the love language of each spouse is seldom the same. Your wife may feel you best show love when you help with the housework or the kids or when you give a surprise gift or offer a compassionate shoulder to cry on. Your husband may feel you best show love when you are intimate or when you compliment him or recognize his achievements. You can find out more on this by reading **The Five Love Languages** by Gary Chapman.

Communicate. Your spouse wants more than anything to feel he or she is your confidant; that you value his or her opinion above all others; that what he or she thinks really matters to you. Avoid excessive criticism at all costs.

Choosing your friends

Make sure you choose your friends wisely and be open to those who want to befriend you.

Be careful not to let relationships, real or

★

imagined, develop around you and suck you in against your will. If they are not intentional and positive, they will drain you.

And, there may be a relationship you want that remains ever out of your reach. Of course, we all know those stories from junior high!

Speaking of junior high, do I have a relationship story for you!! Each year, the first Saturday in November, my junior high school has a reunion. It's a nice event, and I can't attend every year. But, at the November 2015 reunion, I brought glorious closure to the "Billy the Bully" chapter of my life.

"Billy" was the school bully, and I didn't escape his bullying ways. Now this was 1956—junior high in Gastonia, North Carolina. "Billy" and I had been attending the annual reunions for the last ten years. We studiously avoided each other. I admit to having less than charitable feelings toward him. As a child, he was mean to the core. The word "bully" didn't do him justice.

The adult "Billy" had a rough look about him. Nevertheless, he had a pleasant personality, and we both talked to everyone at the reunion—except each other.

In a moment that had to be a divine gift, "Billy" and I wound up at the same table at the same time. Spontaneously, I offered my hand and said, "Hey, Billy!" Using my childhood nickname, he replied, "Hey, Mickey."

★

That was it. But, in that moment, I could feel a tsunami of negative energy leave my body!

In my devotional thought to those attending the reunion, I asked everyone to let go of grudges and forgive those who needed forgiveness. About five minutes later, I got to put that into practice with Billy.

So, that's my message to you: Don't be burdened by those relationships that are still causing you harm. Either make them right or let them go. "Billy" and I will never be soul-brothers, but we are now civil to each other, and I no longer want to throw milk in his face like he did to me in the eighth grade.

In contrast to my "Billy" story, I am reminded of the television sitcom *Cheers* that ran from 1982-1993. The show took place in a Boston bar, and its tagline, "Where everybody knows your name," staked its homey appeal on the notion that there are few sounds more precious to a person than his or her own name.

If you're in conversation or you're working a room and you can't recall a name, listen. People are talking about others. See whom they're talking about and catch that name. Have a wingman with a penchant for names walking with you, giving you a heads-up about who is approaching you with his or her hand extended.

I love to have my wife with me because, unlike me, she is not expected to know everyone, and she introduces herself and gets the person's name in return. And I'm saved.

★

Work the person's name into your conversation. People measure their self-worth in comparison to those they admire. When those they admire recognize them, especially if they call them by name, it boosts them.

You will have relationships of many kinds at many levels. Nurture the ones you want to grow and avoid the ones who would cling to you like barnacles. Be honest and transparent in all of them.

CREATIVITY

No.4

Facing tough problems and
making something new

★

CHAPTER 4

Seizing Creativity with Intention

Creativity requires inspiration.
Inspiration demands action.
Action expresses creativity.
Thus, the magic circle of getting things done.
I live to create. Daytime. . .nighttime. . .dream time.
I love to create. It's fun, hard work, and powerfully
rewarding.

Being asked to speak publicly many times
each month, I have found that creative, dynamic and
inspiring presentations are a must.

Creativity does not occur in a vacuum. It
is called to action by being inspired by a moment,
an event or task that requires something of you.
Inspiration is a divine influence directly exerted
upon the mind or soul. Inspiration is the awakening
of one's being to the songs of the Spirit.

Your personal call to create may not be as the
speaker. You may be asked to present music or a slide

★

show, or to create the table decorations, or to create a parking plan, a printed program. Whatever the opportunity or venue, your presence and participation are required.

That's when you become inspired to take the action to create.

Think of such potential moments: religious service, retirement banquet, annual company event, high school reunion, neighborhood block party — any event that inspires you and therefore triggers your creativity.

You wouldn't have come up with that great speech, funny story, intriguing PowerPoint, or effective plan if there were no inspiring trigger.

Creativity is tied to purpose. And that feeling of having purpose comes along with being inspired.

Before I go further, let me define what I mean by creativity, and then we'll talk about why it's important for your continuing ability to thrive on the peak.

Creativity implies that something new and valuable is being formed — that may be something tangible, such as the items mentioned above, or something intangible, such as a scientific theory, or a joke.

Being inspired to create gives one the ability to transcend traditions, rules, and patterns and be original.

Most often, creative ideas and solutions derive from a fresh view of an old pattern. As the writer of

Ecclesiastes said, "There is nothing new under the sun."

A person inspired to be creative generates or recognizes ideas or possibilities that meet needs. "Creative" implies that these ideas are new, that others have not already thought of or implemented them. They may be new ideas, or a new, original perspective on old ideas or traditions.

Inspiration gives a person the ability to see things that others don't and put things together in combinations that escape others. Inspiration encourages one to find a creative solution.

All who study creativity agree that for something to be considered "creative," it must be more than novel: It must have value, or be appropriate to meet the demands of the situation.

But the beauty is that anyone can be creative. Author Jason Zook says creativity is a muscle. You can build it.

Being creative doesn't necessarily mean being entirely original. A creative person is often one who finds a new combination for existing ideas that builds something never seen before because they were inspired.

More phenomenally, it appears that the ability to be inspired and creative is imbued at birth, and the propensity to create is educated out of us.

In 1968, researcher George Land tested the creativity of 1,600 children. He re-tested the same

★

children when they reached 10 years old and again at 15. Here are the results in the percentage that were deemed "creative."

- Test results amongst 5-year-olds: 98 percent
- Test results amongst 10-year-olds: 30 percent
- Test results amongst 15-year-olds: 12 percent
- Same test given to 280,000 adults: 2 percent

"What we have concluded," Land wrote, "is that non-creative behavior is learned."

Why is it important to be creative if you are going to thrive at the peak? Because the way things have always been done will never move you or your organization into a strong future.

So now, how can you be creative? Do you have a creative gene? Do you need one to be creative?

Fortunately, everyone has the capacity to create. That includes you. Just because you can't sing doesn't mean you can't write a song. If you can't write a novel or even a grade "A" term paper, that doesn't mean you are not creative. If you see yourself that way, it's likely because you've never accepted the challenge to create.

It can be scary to raise your hand and say, "I'll do that," when you know that your audience requires something new. No one wants to bomb.

Some of the most creative people I know took that risk and created something new, something great.

Nido Qubein is president of High Point University in North Carolina. He does not have an earned

★

doctorate. He had no background in higher-education administration. He is a businessman and motivational speaker.

Yet, he has taken a little Southern school to the top of the regional college lists in **US News and World Report**. He's raised hundreds of millions of dollars, doubled enrollment, tripled endowment, and completely rebuilt the campus.

Qubein came to the United States from Lebanon at age 15 with $3.00 in his pocket and no command of English. He exudes creativity and new ideas with every breath.

Another creative, transformational personality is Oprah Winfrey. Chances are that you know her story of poverty and abuse, rising above it to create literally her OWN television network. Almost everything she touches turns to gold.

At the height of her afternoon talk show, she could spike a book's sales by 50,000 by making it her book club selection. She is about lifting women, helping little girls in Africa, and making a difference. She is doing it by constantly creating and re-creating herself.

In an affirmation of my belief that creativity stems from meeting a real need, Bill Gates created the largest personal fortune in the world by creating the software that runs the majority of the world's computers.

In recent years, he's removed himself from

★

active daily management of Microsoft and is devoting his attention to the Bill and Melinda Gates Foundation, which they created to address health and education issues around the globe. They have also created awareness in the minds of many of the nation's wealthiest individuals that they have an opportunity and an obligation to put their money to work philanthropically.

What is a common denominator among these creative people? Their responses to specific needs have enabled them to influence a tremendous number of others. Their solutions solve problems. Their creativity is not an effervescent idea drawn from thin air only to expand and burst like a bubble.

One of the most creative people I've observed is Linda Morgan, a long-term staff member. She never stops—serving children and families through Baptist Children's Homes is her life.

She creates opportunities for fun. She dresses up for holidays, cultivates relationships, and digs potatoes every year when her group visits a local farmer who donates them to us. She is always thinking of ways to improve service and to generate excitement. She is a known and trusted individual and team member.

People will allow you to be creative and follow your creative ideas if they trust you.

In recent days, several people have told me they keep their financial commitment to BCH going because, they said, "We trust you." My most valuable currency is the trust of our constituencies.

A team likes a creative leader. A team appreciates someone who is creative and dynamic and puts them on the frontier where firsts can be found.

My priority is staff, because through them I multiply myself. If I can make life better for staff, then they can make life better for children. I want to see that they have a good salary, good benefits, access to leadership, and a good working environment. I want them to feel good about their work, to be happy and secure so they can give the children all they've got.

To do that, I've got to stay creative. Here are some of the ways I manage that, even after a third of a century in the same role.

- **Find a quiet place.** Leaders are inundated with calls, emails, alerts, visitors, snail mail, meetings, and deadlines. We have more information being thrown at us than we can sort, analyze and absorb. Yet, when was the last time a creative idea surfaced in your brain while you were neck deep in your inbox? Give yourself time and space to create.
- **Be willing to throw away your first brilliant idea.** While it was good enough to post on Facebook when it popped into your mind, after you mull it over for a while you realize it wasn't that good and it's got to go.
- **Pay attention.** At a recent leadership event,

I worked the room before the program started. Then I listened closely to what went on before it was my time to speak. I was able to interject lots of spontaneous comments from things I'd learned earlier in the morning.

Spontaneity is enabled by your comfort with the audience and confidence in yourself. Confidence allows you to be creative, which in turn should lead to an increase in comfort and more confidence.

You don't like to "work the room?" Remember, they want you to succeed. They're on your side. Part of that is selfish because they don't want to be bored for the next hour! Just introduce yourself. Most people will be glad the speaker has come off the dais to introduce him or herself—it creates a connection.

- **Whatever it is you're working on, do it out loud.** How does it sound? How does it look? Does it resonate? Is it truly your voice? Does it sound phony? Are the illustrations yours, or have you cribbed them? If the illustration fits your point, you can use it, but be sure to give attribution. Crediting the original author does not make your remarks any less legitimate. In fact, it increases legitimacy because it tells the audience that you are well-read and that what you are saying is backed up by more than just your opinion.
- **Read a lot.** Read novels, nonfiction, newspapers, magazines. Read road signs

★

and billboards. Read the labels on your food. The world is full of ideas. You won't build a sandbox from any one thing you read, but each will contribute a grain. I don't like to be in conversation when someone mentions an idea or event that's in the news and I don't have any idea what they're talking about.

• **Be patient.** Wait for the spirit to either inform or affirm what you're doing. Wait for that moment of illumination/inspiration.

• **Write it down.** Take notes. Part of my creativity is to jot down notes on scraps of paper. When I think of something, I have to get it down lest I forget. For years I've had a pen and pad by the bed. I now supplement that by typing notes into my phone.

• **Know your creative time.** Mine is in the morning. I like to vocalize and stretch in the morning, opening up the pipes for blood flow.

• **Eat well.** To function at my best requires adequate rest and good nutrition. I'm not saying, "Eat a lot." I'm saying eat well. Eat real food, not processed food. It's better to skip a meal than to fill your body with junk.

I no longer indiscriminately eat dessert. Dessert is like an addictive substance for me. Recently, I was returning home from a four-day business trip when I drove past BBQ Joe's at 8:45 p.m. I knew BBQ Joe's didn't close until 9 p.m. and I also knew that BBQ

★

Joe's had the best brownies in the universe.

I bought three brownies; two for that night and one for the morning. I was like an addict. Addicted mice will choose sugar over cocaine, and I understand that. I knew better, but time and circumstances colluded to enable me to justify wheeling into BBQ Joe's.

Hey, if God had meant me not to go there, He would have had the restaurant already be closed when I drove past, right? Those three brownies cost me five pounds. They kept me from getting my red jacket at Structure House's Success Week.

The red jacket at Structure House is like the green jacket awarded the winner of the Masters Golf Tournament. It signifies that the wearer has lost 100 pounds and has gained control of destructive habits that lead to overeating and ill health.

On June 28, 2004, when I stepped on the scales at Structure House for the first time, they groaned upward until the indicator stopped at 328.4 lbs. I moved at the speed of a sloth. My knees hurt, I seldom had enough breath, and I was easily influenced by church ladies who offered this big-eating preacher a sample of their prizewinning pie — or the whole pie.

Those brownies really cost me at the weigh-in, at which I expected to get my jacket. It was during a special week at Structure House, and many people I've worked with over the years would have been present. But at 233.2 pounds, I missed the 100-pound mark and the jacket.

★

I've since earned the jacket — awarded in a balloon-filled ceremony with lots of the encouragement, affirmation and a huge slice of watermelon with the number "101" planted on top.

- **Keep your mind clear.** Some people could write when they were drunk, or sleep-deprived, or sugared-out. If I were in any of those conditions, I couldn't be creative. I could barely muddle through it. For me to be creative, I've got to be clear-headed. That means if I'm fatigued, I'll take a nap. There's no need to fight it. A nap is restorative.
- **Be intentional about it.** Try to do something every day that could be a source for a new thought or a fresh perspective. Read something from somebody of another viewpoint.
- **Seek and put yourself in the midst of stimulating company.** When you're talking and sharing ideas with energetic, thoughtful people, your own creative juices flow. Somewhere, somehow flint strikes steel and a spark ignites for mutual benefit.

The truth is, if you're running the ridge of success, you're already creative. The mandate is to sustain it, so you must never let the creative gene go dormant.

I recently was in a regional meeting in which Nido Qubein made a presentation. I got fired up from his address, and I'll tell you, it takes a lot to fire me

★

up because I've been to lots of seminars and conferences.

His remark that struck me most is that "the day of average is over." That's the way I think. We don't do average at BCH!

In becoming president of an old entity in 1983, I had to follow my own light. Sure, I had to study hard to learn the history and the present of this institution. But I saw the iceberg and I knew the future demanded another course.

I still follow my own light, and when I gain a new light, I follow it. A new light told me shortly after I started as president that to be successful into the future, BCH must serve not only children, but also the families from which they came. The new light said we were going to have to diversify, expand our services.

When you read, study, give yourself a quiet place and cogitate on a thought, a new light appears and you follow it. There's a crack in everything; that's how the light comes in.

I love to follow politics. At one time, I was interested in holding political office, but I realized I could get more meaningful things done where I am. Here I have the authority to let my imagination find expression.

One of the most creative things I've ever done was early in my ministry when we started the college outreach at Ridge Road Baptist Church in Raleigh.

★

This was in 1970 when I was 28.

I was minister for youth and college students but we had no college students. We were just a mile or so from a church with an outstanding college ministry, primarily to students from North Carolina State University. We had nothing.

It started with some freshmen from NC State and from nearby all-female Meredith College. Eventually, we had more than 100 every Sunday. It was hard work—creative work—and among the most rewarding I've ever done.

I was able to motivate adults in the church to help, which was a key to success, along with the 10 dozen Krispy Kreme doughnuts I provided at the highly-discounted cost of $4.80 each week. I got the address of every incoming freshman from Meredith and NC State and wrote them a personal note. They never forgot that.

We started a coffee house in a building adjacent to the church. We had 200 on opening night. It was a creative venture that carried a high risk that some church members would not understand what we were doing. Our continued operation of the coffee house actually came to a vote and this unique outreach ministry was overwhelming approved.

That was a period of my creativity backed with passion and an ability to get people to do what I wanted them to do. It was the first time I realized I had leadership potential.

★

After I left that church staff to become a pastor, I met with my students from those years annually for probably 15 straight years. Several are in ministry careers and one is on my board now.

Nothing requires creativity like starting something from nothing.

When North Carolina Baptists shifted their focus for ministry among a rapidly-aging population away from residential facilities, they asked Baptist Children's Homes to come up with a plan — and to be responsible for whatever we created.

I was humbled when denominational leaders looked to BCH, and to me, as the logical leader for such an effort. They recognized that I had earned the trust of the people who would be asked to fund it.

This was an opportunity to put a stamp on something completely new: There was no template, no model and no precedent. This would be pure, utter, 100 percent creativity. In other words, I salivated.

We brainstormed and imagined. We came up with a name that itself exudes energy: NCBAM. That stands for North Carolina Baptist Aging Ministry. It's beginning to take off now. We hear people say, "That NCBAM thing is really good."

We've gone from nothing to providing year-round service for hundreds of frail elderly adults that enables them to stay in their homes. Our staff is minimal, and its primary function is to organize

★

volunteer labor across the state, with the hands-on labor being provided by local church volunteers.

All these volunteers needed was a central clearinghouse, which we provide, and off they go to minister.

We're growing and expanding the influence of NCBAM to do good things. We sponsor a conference every year for retired ministers. We help with conferences for aging that other entities conduct. We've established three Aging Adults Innovative Ministries (AAIM) regions as a subset of NCBAM. We help churches establish better senior adult ministries.

We had a mandate to meet a specific need. BAM(!) — that's when the creative juices flow and good things arise from nothing.

The social conditions that called Baptist Children's Homes into existence in 1885 did not remain stagnant. Through the decades we've had to develop services and create ministries — in addition to traditional residential care — to meet changing needs.

We began a home for teen mothers and their babies; a ministry to developmentally disabled adults; family care for hard-working moms and their children; early childhood education; specialized group homes; and outdoor year-round camping programs for both boys and girls who build their own shelters while learning self-reliance. We've established a relationship with an orphanage in Guatemala and helped sister institutions in Brazil.

★

Timing is everything. I had been approached many times over the years by elderly parents with adult children who were mentally unable to live by themselves. The parents' greatest concern was what would happen to their children when the parents were no longer around to care for them.

With much investigation and some seed money, we established one by one a network of homes where these adults can live and age together with caring supervision. When the brass ring comes around, you've got to grab it.

That was one good idea that has come to fruition. I've had ideas I thought were good that didn't go anywhere.

If your emotional makeup says you are easily discouraged if your ideas don't go anywhere, you're going to have a hard time pushing a creative idea. And sometimes, they do need to be pushed. Even good ideas that are just "offered" can float away like puffs of cattail seeds on the wind.

Mastery of the creative process is rarely an accident. What is absolutely critical is to be aware that:

- *Creativity requires inspiration.*
- *Inspiration demands action.*
- *Action expresses creativity.*

★

Striving for vigor and soundness
of body, mind and spirit

★

★ ★ ★

★

CHAPTER 5

Reaching Your Optimum You

Do you possess anything more valuable than your health?

For too long, I regarded my health as a given. I treated my body with disregard and was inconsistent with what I put into it and what I required of it. In return, it was threatening to derail all that I had worked for.

If you are going to run with the ibex on the ridge, pay attention to your health—now.

By 1994, I had been president of Baptist Children's Homes of North Carolina for 11 years. The work was relentless, and I seldom took a break of long enough duration ever to relax.

I ate my way through both stress and celebration and desperately needed the three-month sabbatical my trustees offered me that year.

I retreated to Episcopal Seminary in Virginia, a sojourn that included days of quietude and medita-

★

tion. The enforced silence squeezed like shackles around a voluble person like me. But too seldom do any of us come to a halt long enough to listen, to close our mouths and open our ears, and then to meditate on "what is."

It was a pivotal experience.

The following year, I was to return as an alumnus to share with the current participants any epiphany of my own retreat. I took up the offer of BCH benefactor Paul Broyhill for time at his house to cogitate, think, pray, and meditate about what I'd learned.

I had been incorporating into my life revelations from my own retreat, but I had not defined them into a digestible system of thought. From those days in the Broyhill home I defined the three prongs of my new healthful lifestyle: diet, exercise and meditation.

Diet: You are what you eat

No single factor determines your health more than what you put into your mouth.

Plain and simple, you are what you eat.

Twentieth century nutritionist Victor Lindlahr believed that food controls health and wrote in 1923, "Ninety percent of the diseases known to man are caused by cheap foodstuffs. You are what you eat."

I've known this most of my life, kind of in the way I knew Mount Everest is tall or that the queen lives in England. It's a fact, but a tidbit that somehow was never taken seriously by me.

★

I grew up with three basic food groups: sugar, salt and fat.

My mother was overweight, and I was her only child. She was a good cook in that she made tasty dishes. She believed in clean plates. She convinced me the "hungry children in China" sat in judgment of my every leftover scoop of mashed potatoes.

Unlike Mom and me, when my dad was full he could slide his chair away from the dinner table with a word of appreciation — "Enjoyed it" — even when some food remained on his plate. Then he'd step outside for a smoke.

If I called his attention to the fact that he left some food uneaten, he said, "Give it to your mother."

My young and impressionable mind believed my only option was a clean plate, and mom was a good cook. Draw your own conclusions.

But I kept active and at six-feet tall, 190 pounds at high school graduation was not out of bounds.

Still, I was already conscious of my weight, and, I actually popped my first diet pill in high school. They didn't become a habit, but looking back I understand the pressure even then to conform to a certain body image.

I didn't have the same pressures to eat everything while in college at Chapel Hill. In fact, I lost 20 pounds. Besides being active in campus life, I worked at the dining hall to get a free meal. I wanted to be a journalist and worked hard on the *Daily Tar Heel* staff.

★

I worked harder there than in the classroom, and loved it.

I loved the beautiful Chapel Hill campus of the University of North Carolina, too. And I walked everywhere, always aware that walking was good for me. No doubt I did my share of moaning and groaning having to cross the large campus on foot, especially when I was scurrying to meet a deadline. But the walking kept me healthy and feeling good.

Real world stress hit me once I graduated and started working two jobs. My response? Comfort food.

Fifty pounds piled onto my frame and took me up to 240 pounds before I knew what was happening. And I hadn't gotten any taller.

The interests that captivated me drove me to succeed, to excel, to pursue with all my energy, those interests that captivated me. When I felt a call to the ministry, rather than a career in broadcasting, I enrolled in seminary even while anchoring the news at a Raleigh television station. I added a part-time church staff role to that mix, and soon I was catching myself coming and going.

This was real life now. It all counted, and I felt driven to conquer every mountain. Lack of sleep, demands of school and work while trying to be a good husband and feeling like I was "on stage" in every area of life raised my stress quotient to dangerous levels.

My prescription was comfort food. Under stress, I ate. It didn't matter what—anything to put into my

★

mouth. The sensation of food and the taste of something sweet or salty would calm me.

When I was my most careless self, I could eat a dozen Krispy Kreme donuts at one sitting. Once during a vacation week in a period of high stress, I ate a quart of ice cream every day and tablespoon after tablespoon of peanut butter.

I once stopped at the fast food joint Cook Out and got three milk shakes. I drank one on the way home, and walked in the door with the remaining two and told my wife, "Look, I got us each a shake."

When I was pastor in Carthage, NC, graduated from seminary, and down to one job, I caught on to the running craze. I ran every day, sometimes twice a day. I knew all about the runner's high, and I craved a daily fix.

Then one night I stepped into a hole in the street and sprained my ankle. My running days were over and my eating days returned.

I had the good fortune to meet Gerard Musante in 1975. He was a healthy- lifestyle guru and diet expert. He recognized that a diet is not something you're "on" but something you "have."

He ran a program at Duke University to which I faithfully went every week for a group session. It cost $20 each week (lunch included), and he designed a healthy, weight loss diet for me on which I dropped 52 pounds. I was never happier than at that time. A structured lifestyle and diet felt good!

★

Studies have shown that preachers are among the least healthy segment of the population. And Baptist preachers, so I've heard, are the least healthy of that group.

But know that weight management affects everything about your health and well-being: blood pressure, joint pain, stamina, and zest for living.

Adopt this discipline early in your career and you won't have to endure the yo-yo battle with weight that kept me wound up for so many years.

After a pastorate in Richmond, I became president of Baptist Children's Homes of North Carolina in 1983. Immediately I was submerged in a tidal wave of work to try to get this ocean liner moving through the waves again. BCH had a marvelous, effective history of almost 100 years, but it had lost momentum, and no one seemed aware that it was listing.

The centennial was upon us in 1985. My first two years required endless hours to get my arms around our mission, all while positioning us to capitalize on the natural publicity and marketing opportunities of our centennial.

I worked night and day, eating my way through the stress. And when the centennial was behind us, I celebrated with more food. By 1987, I started getting myself back under control, but the workload was unrelenting. I didn't take a significant break until my sabbatical in 1994.

That was a pivotal time for me. I recommend

a sabbatical for physical, emotional, mental, and spiritual renewal and I urge institutions of worship to offer one to every staff member after a predetermined period of service.

My diet, exercise and meditation revelation may not be unique. It's not something I sat down and scratched out on a piece of paper because I had to have something to turn in. It revealed itself like a butterfly crawling wet and colorful from its cocoon once I secreted myself away to a place where I could see it.

Ten years later, I got careless and began to spin out of control concerning my weight. I took a month off to attend the residential program that Musante had started in Durham called Structure House.

He asked, "What's eating you?" and showed me a psychological approach to weight management. I was obviously eating for the wrong reasons and needed to look at behaviors and triggers.

Structure House was a remarkable place for a guy like me. I lived there a month in an environment totally devoted to recalibrating me to health.

There, you are all in: no sugar, caffeine, fat, salt. Your body will probably go through withdrawal. In my 2004 immersion, I had three days of headaches.

I still go back for tune-ups. That's my vacation. Some people take trips to the beach or go on a cruise. I take a week at Structure House.

Every day is exercise, swimming, training, nutrition, classes, education about the real reasons you

★

overeat, and modifications put into place to address those issues.

My first time really turned me around, but I'm still constantly working out my relationship with food. I have a diet but I might reward myself with a special treat. That would not include ice cream because if I have a scoop, I'll want the pint. I can't do that.

That said, be careful about deprivation diets. If you declare something is "off-limits" you may get fixated on the self-denial. Remember Adam and Eve in the Garden of Eden? They could have anything in the garden—anything—except to eat from the tree of the knowledge of good and evil. On what did they fixate?

Be wary of your trigger foods and avoid them. It is simpler never to put one to your lips than to wrestle with the demon as it courses through your body. A trigger food will set you off on a path that goes only downhill.

I just told you one of mine is ice cream. Sugar begets sugar, and one chocolate chip cookie begets another. That's biblical, right?

It's not that these foods are forbidden to you. No food is forbidden to you. It's that you consciously decide not to eat them. I don't remember the last time I ordered dessert at a restaurant. I find if I'm with a group and no one orders dessert, no one orders dessert.

You can be the first "no one," and your fellow diners will bless you.

★

Exercise: No excuses

You are without excuse.

I've heard them all and used them all.

But, we have no excuse not to exercise. None.

Don't have time? Take time to do something that will make you healthier, more effective at work, happier in mood, better able to maintain your weight, and generally keep you a more pleasant person to be around!

Canadian neuroscientist Brian Christie rides a bike to the gym, then to work. When he gets there, he says his brain is at "peak activity for a few hours." When he feels himself tailing off, he rides to finish some errands.

Selene Yeager is a professional cyclist who writes as the Fit Chick in **Bicycling** magazine. She told Christie's story in a 2015 issue and examined the "scientifically proven" premise that exercise boosts brainpower and emotional health.

"Exercise is like fertilizer for your brain," Yeager wrote. Working out boosts capillary growth in your brain and muscles, which means more oxygen and nutrients get to them to help them work.

Scientists writing in the **Journal of Clinical and Diagnostic Research** found that people finished faster and scored higher on tests of memory, reasoning, and planning after 30 minutes of spinning on a stationary bike.

Exercise forces more nerve cells to fire and

intensify creation of proteins like brain-derived neurotrophic factor (BDNF) and a protein called noggin (NOG), which promote formation of new brain cells.

"You are literally building your brain," said Christie.

This is a vitally important aspect to consider since your brain shrinks as you age and those connections weaken. Arthur Kramer, a neuroscientist at the University of Illinois, said his research shows that exercise restores and protects the brain.

A bigger, more connected brain simply works better, Yeager wrote.

Now, that doesn't mean if a little is good, that longer, harder, higher, tougher is automatically better. The sweet spot for mental acuity benefits is 30-60 minutes of moderate to intense work at about 75 percent of maximum ability.

In other words, it's better to exercise a little every day than to be a weekend warrior and run a marathon or cycle 100 miles.

And when it comes to emotional health, exercise works as well as, or maybe even better, than psychotherapy and antidepressants to ward off depression, according to James Blumenthal, professor of behavioral medicine at Duke University. His study analyzing 26 years of research finds that 20-30 minutes of exercise daily can prevent depression over the long term.

The Federal Centers for Disease Control in

Atlanta says sedentary living — not high cholesterol as you might suspect — is the nation's leading culprit in fatal heart attacks.

Exercise conquers a sedentary lifestyle, and it requires no prescription or special equipment.

Coronary disease accounts for about 27 percent of the 2.1 million deaths among Americans each year. Sedentary people are about twice as likely to die from a heart attack as people who are physically active.

According to an article in the Raleigh **News & Observer**, researchers consider people sedentary who either do no purposeful physical activity or who exercise less than three times a week or less than 20 minutes at a time, or both.

What does exercise do?

It can lower blood levels of artery-damaging LDL cholesterol while raising beneficial HDL cholesterol. A study of 3,621 adults published in the September 2014 issue of **The American Journal of Public Health** showed that those who walked for exercise for at least four and a half hours a week were half as likely to have unfavorable cholesterol levels as people who walked only a half-hour to two hours a week.

Physically active people who suffer a heart attack are more likely to survive it.

Regular physical exercise can help to lower blood pressure without medication, which reduces your chances of suffering a stroke or developing kidney disease.

Many diabetics who exercise regularly and follow a proper diet can reduce — or in some cases eliminate — their dependence on insulin or other medications.

Exercise can help to curb excessive stress reactions and speed the return to normal when stress becomes an unavoidable burden.

An American College of Sports Medicine opinion paper on physical fitness recommendations for adults said exercise should be rhythmic and aerobic using large muscle groups. Examples are walking, jogging, bicycling, rowing, and stair climbing.

It also recommended adding resistance training with the use of free weights, weight machines or calisthenics to increase or maintain muscular strength and endurance.

Any other obstacles?

• *"I don't have time."*

Then take the stairs instead of the elevator. Park away from the entrance and walk 100 yards. Set your clock 10 minutes earlier and walk around the block. Turn off the television and play catch with the kids. Instead of "movie night," go bowling or play Frisbee or explore a park.

You would be amazed at how small your neighborhood really is when you walk it. Sometimes we think things are a car trip away because we just always go out and "get in the car." If you are a half-mile from the grocery, that's just a 10 minute walk.

★

You know it takes you that long to find your keys, get into the car, ease into traffic, wait at the light, cruise the parking lot three times looking for a spot near the entrance, and then make your way to the door.

We make time for whatever we want to make time for. Your priorities come first—that's what defines them as priorities. If the president of the United States finds time to exercise every day, you can.

Sure, it's hard to do sometimes. I didn't feel like it yesterday. But I knew if I didn't do it, I wasn't going to feel well. I like feeling good, so I dragged myself to the gym and, as always, slapped the sloth right out of my bones.

Since becoming an advocate of activity, I developed a workshop for my staff to encourage them to find five minutes a day to move. "Move, move," went the refrain. "Five minutes a day—you've got to find your groove and move, move, move!"

There are certain exercises I do before I speak, to relax my body and voice; staff encouraged me to share them with the trustees before one meeting. So I had them lift their arms over their heads and say, "Wheeeee."

They followed right along, and we all had a great time. This is not something I ever would have done earlier in my tenure, but that's another part of the freedom I'm enjoying now running along this ridge.

I can be more spontaneous. I've always been able to think on my feet, but for so many years I withheld spontaneous reactions, things that might have livened up a conversation or event, so I could maintain the "dignity" of my office.

Now I realize that people really like to see the president with the robes of propriety lowered to reveal an authentic and human man behind the title.

• "I don't have money."

How much does it take? Go outside and walk. That's the best single exercise you can do anyway. You don't need to buy fancy Lycra pants, bright colored shoes, mats, bikes, power-output monitors, mesh jerseys or club memberships. Just step outside and walk around the block in the shoes you're wearing.

Take the first step, and live more joyfully and healthfully.

• "I don't have a place to exercise."

You live somewhere. Sit down on the floor and do a sit-up. Sit on a chair and lift your arms. Step outside the door and walk to the end of the driveway or around the block.

Join a local YMCA or find a place with workout facilities. They often offer exercise classes for the community.

• "I'm not healthy enough to exercise."

Say what? Getting started with exercise is an early step to regaining your health. It will do more for you than many of the pills you may be taking, I promise. I'm not offering you medical advice here, and you

★

should tell your doctor you're ready to start getting some exercise. (I'm also aware that many people cannot exercise because of severe physical limitations).

I promise she/he will be thrilled to hear your intentions. People all around me who have started exercising and watching their diets have been able to stop taking certain blood pressure and blood sugar medicine.

Against my fear of offering you an excuse, I will caution you not to overdo it at first. Not because your heart is going to blow up and splatter your walls red, but because if you overdo it to start, you'll be sore and you'll use that for an excuse to "wait a few days" before you do any exercise again.

"Waiting a few days" is the devil on your shoulder saying, "We're all done here." You won't define "a few," and "days" become months.

The best thing you can do after the first exercise that makes your muscles sore is to exercise again with the sore muscles. They'll loosen up, and your soreness will actually be shorter term.

When I finally committed to exercise, I took advantage of a special deal at the local Y and got a trainer. A trainer isn't magic, and a trainer is not going to make you do or enable you to do anything you couldn't do without one.

But, a trainer can show you how to use the equipment, teach you some exercises and supervise so you do them correctly and don't hurt yourself. And,

★

the trainer's biggest benefit is your accountability. Having a trainer — or an exercise partner — gets you out there.

Besides keeping me accountable to be regular, my trainer helps me with my flexibility. He pushes and pulls to help me stretch, and shows me movements to help my balance. Flexibility is important to maintain as we age.

Remember, I'm encouraging you in these areas so that you grab the benefits sooner than I did. When you exercise you feel better, you perform better, you have a better perspective on life, are less likely to be depressed, and you are healthier.

Since I've committed to diet, exercise and meditation, I don't keep any fat clothes in my closet. When I lost weight from my peak of 328.4 pounds, I cleansed not only my body, but also my closet. There are no reminders of what I used to be and no "welcome back" suits for a return visit. Today, I weigh 237.4 or a sustained weight loss of 101 pounds. My "red jacket" ceremony at Structure House included a "surprise" slice of watermelon with 101 prominently displayed for all the celebrants to see.

You need your own exercise regimen, determined after you've educated yourself, and in consultation with a doctor if you are far from healthy. But just to give you an idea, my current regimen is an hour of cardio four days a week. I'm 74, so my cardio is not rock-wall climbing or sprinting up sand dunes

★

pulling a 100-lb bag of rocks.

I walk, either on a treadmill or a stair-stepper or around a track. If time is an issue, I simply step outside my door and walk the neighborhood. An added benefit is that walking your neighborhood is a good way to meet your neighbors.

I lift weights at least twice a week to retain the muscle mass we lose naturally as we age. Flexibility is important, so I do stretching exercises and occasional yoga.

I'm never going to be 170 pounds, and don't want to be. I'd look funny. I have too much scalp for that weight.

Without exercise, I could never maintain my 101-lb weight loss. I'm committed to staying as far away as I can from the sluggish, big, clumsy, self-conscious guy I've been. When I was at my biggest, I wasn't myself. There was more of me, but I wasn't "the me" who is now free to run the ridge and sustain success at the peak!

Meditation: Get in touch with yourself

Although I'm going to devote the least amount of space to this part of the triad—diet, exercise and meditation—that doesn't diminish its importance. For you, it may be the most important of the three.

The Judeo-Christian tradition may define meditation as seeking the mind of God or searching for the presence of Spirit. It is a personal practice for me, and I encourage you to do it.

★

But, unlike those who say you can pray anywhere, you cannot meditate while driving the car, or golfing, or fishing or throwing a baseball with your kids.

You must set yourself apart from the demands of your life. Jerk yourself from the gravitational pull of every little planet that insists you orbit around it.

Meditation can be, and sometimes is, silent prayer for me. I'm not verbalizing thoughts, but waiting for whatever the Spirit impresses on me.

Take a moment, catch your breath, hear yourself breathe. Inhale slowly and hold the breath, then exhale slowly.

I use a phone app that creates relaxing background noise for me. "Noise" is an insufficient word to describe the relaxing, centering effectiveness of the sounds of a mountain brook, or rain on a roof, or breezes over grasslands. But it's not music. It is broad and indistinct enough that my mind does not focus on it, but rather it brushes out other distractions.

Recently when my anxiety was through the roof, I dialed up the sounds of rain on leaves. I let it play while I just laid down. Before, I might have roamed the kitchen in search of something to eat.

I don't use food to calm me much anymore. I'm not totally sugar celibate, but now I'm the one in control, not the little sirens singing from Sugar Island.

Beyond spiritual life, meditation includes more of an intentional mindfulness of your moments. We

★

rush through life to get to the next thing. In the rush, we gobble food, slight relationships and relinquish to the insignificant more command of our life than it deserves.

Mindfulness doesn't just mean slow down. It means cultivating awareness to a higher degree, being mindful of your environment and your activity. Tell yourself to walk down the sidewalk and not step on a crack. Suddenly, you're mindful that the sidewalk is made of sections. It is hard beneath your feet. You see the sections are not perfectly level and might even be upended where a tree's roots grew beneath them and fattened.

If you are eating mindfully, you taste, savor and enjoy each bite. You're not just eating lunch; you're eating a salad. The salad has individual elements. The arugula tastes different from the spinach. The peas are overcooked, and the carrots could have used a little more steam.

You don't drown all the elements with a dressing so that everything tastes "ranch."

The concept of mindfulness is mainstream now. It's everywhere you look. Be aware, slow down, move away from the frantic pace.

Taste your food. Feel its texture and temperature.

I don't do fast food anymore, unless it's a potato and chili at Wendy's. If I wanted a French fry, I could have one. But I'd be happy with one. I'd savor it.

Think of life in terms of savoring it. Each meal is

★

a gift, each day an adventure, each moment a treasure. When you race through life, you race through meals; you miss moments, days, entire weeks. You devour your precious allocation of time with no appreciation.

Mindfulness allows me actually to enjoy and celebrate what I'm eating. This meal is sufficient. This meal provides me the nutrients and energy I need to get to my next task or next meal.

If you eat beyond that, that's probably the excess that becomes fat. If you eat slowly you really do fill up with less food. It takes 20 minutes for your body to register "full" to your brain. So you can be beyond full before you're aware you need to stop eating.

Think of all those holiday meals where we push away from the table barely able to stumble to the sofa and feeling miserable the rest of the afternoon.

Jon Kabat-Zinn, professor of medicine emeritus at the University of Massachusetts Medical School, is an early and prominent writer in the field of mindfulness. He created the Stress Reduction Clinic and the Center for Mindfulness in Medicine, Health Care, and Society.

To him, "Mindfulness means paying attention in a particular way; on purpose, in the present moment, and nonjudgmentally."

When you begin to live with mindfulness, your moments will count.

Together, they will build a life.

★

LAUGHTER

No. 6

The antidote to anger and hostility

★

★ ★ ★

CHAPTER 6

Laughing Your Way to Success

"When I die, I want to die like my grandfather who died peacefully in his sleep. Not screaming like all the passengers in his car." (Will Rogers)

Laughter slices the tension at many meetings or in difficult relationships. It's hard to be mad at someone with whom you're laughing. Who can be pessimistic when you can find something to laugh about and see the humor in things?

If for no other reason, we need to laugh because it literally is good for us. Laughter boosts our immune system.

You may know the story of journalist Norman Cousins. He once got very sick, which, while awful, put him on his back with lots of time to read. In his reading he learned a lot about how negative emotions damage the body and spirit, and he determined to fight the negative emotions that seemed to well up in him due to his circumstances.

★

So he hired a nurse to read him funny stories. He watched Marx Brothers movies. He looked for laughs and found that laughter relieved pain and helped him sleep.

Ultimately, he wrote about his experience in **The Anatomy of an Illness**, which was met with much skepticism, even derision, by his cardigan-clad colleagues. But finally, in 1989, the **Journal of the American Medical Association** acknowledged that laughter therapy could help improve the quality of life for patients with chronic illness. Laughter had an immediate symptom-relieving effect with the ability to strengthen the human immune system.

Mark Twain said this about laughter: "The human race has only one really effective weapon, and that's laughter. The moment it arises, all our hardnesses yield, all our irritations and resentments slip away and a sunny spirit takes their place."

Dr. Michael Miller, in his book with Catherine Knepper, **Heal Your Heart**, said one of his favorite moments as a physician is when he tells patients the one thing they absolutely must do to ensure a successful recovery is to "go home and laugh until they cry."

A big reason for this instruction is that unresolved stress directly contributes to heart disease. Anger and hostility lead to stress, and laughter is an antidote to those harmful emotions.

"Deep laughter triggers the release of endorphins, which activate receptors in our blood vessels' linings that signal the production of nitric oxide," he wrote. "This powerful chemical causes blood vessel dilation, increases blood flow and reduces vascular inflammation."

"Laugh hysterically," he said.

During a study in which he had people watch clips of both a war movie and a comedy, he found that participants' blood vessels were narrowing by up to 50 percent during the stressful war segments, while vessel dilation in people who watched a funny clip increased 22 percent. The vascular benefit of 15 minutes of laughter, he said, was the same as 15 to 30 minutes at the gym.

Laughter doesn't take the place of conventional treatment, but it sure is a good adjunctive therapy. It's natural as sunshine and comes with no negative side effects.

Speaking of side effects, what do you think of those drug commercials on television that take twice as long to list potential negative consequences as they do to describe the medicine's benefits? I laugh out loud as the voice-over drones on more about the drug's potential to cause harm than it does about its chances heal you.

Take this pill to alleviate the common cold, the TV ad intones. Then listen to the announcer warn you about possible side effects such as unsightly rash on the left cheek bone; fever leading to either chattering chills or night sweats; unusual tongue swelling which

★

can limit your ability to laugh and which can only
be relieved by a large scoop of Ben and Jerry's Cherry
Garcia ice cream; or, in rare cases, binge watching of
old episodes of "Matlock" or "I Love Lucy."

Reader's Digest doesn't call laughter "the best
medicine" for nothing. The iconic monthly magazine
of brief stories, observations, anecdotes and humor
will pay you if they use a funny story that you send
them. They know good jokes attract readers because
people want to laugh. Even if we can't describe why
laughter is good for us, we know it is because we
feel better when we do it.

At 74, I've had lots of birthdays. But only one
birthday brought with it the sense that life was over,
done with, finished with nothing left to accomplish.
That was May 3, 2002—the day I turned 60.

I sat in my office, blinds drawn. I was sullen,
grumpy and depressed, knowing I couldn't pretend
to be young anymore. I determined to just sit there
all day and feel sorry for myself—even though that
birthday relieved me of one of the great worries that
many people live with—I no longer had to be worried
about dying young!

Suddenly, there was a ruckus and pounding
on my door. Outside, a staff member escorted me to
a vintage automobile and took me to a surprise party
where middle-aged women were dressed up like
teenagers and danced in poodle skirts to songs from
the late 50s and early 60s—the generation of my

★

youth. I laughed for an hour. My self-pitying
depression lifted and my spirits soared as high
and free as those 60 helium-filled balloons.

I've never dreaded a birthday since.

In fact, believe it or not, I couldn't wait to turn
70. It was the second greatest year of my life, second
only to the one I'm living right now.

There are all kinds of humor. Some things
make you smirk like you're the only one who gets the
inside joke, or the unintended double entendre. Sometimes you smile big and bright because you're happy
to hear a story, or you just enjoyed watching the
person tell it because it obviously so tickled the teller.
Sometimes you hear something so outrageous or un-
expected or so "I'm glad it was you and not me" kind
of funny that you laugh out loud—from your toes to
your nose with your belly shaking in the middle.

Big belly laughs are rare, especially as you gain
lots of life experience. It's just harder to surprise you.
You've heard it, seen it, done it, recovered from it
already. I find humor in many things, but I admit
I don't often land on a laugh that shakes me.

I love when my 9-year-old granddaughter,
Piper, says something funny. Maybe she tells me
a joke from a joke book I've given her, and I just
love that she delights in telling it to me, never
suspecting I've heard it before. Or she'll make up
jokes, or share jokes she's heard from friends and
may not even understand.

★

Little children's jokes are just so simple and fun that you laugh just to hear them share: Why did the horse cross the road? He wanted to see his NAAAYYbors.

Spontaneous hilarity, grammatically incorrect sentences, misspeaking a word that results in saying a word with a different meaning that doesn't fit in her sentence, and she dies laughing. Laughter is contagious, and when she laughs, I laugh.

Her laughter contains no shame, no self-consciousness. She, like many of us, is her own best audience, and when she tickles herself, she'll tell me, "That's hilarious, Boppy." And you know something? It really is.

I can't remember jokes. Someone may tell a joke that makes me laugh and I'll want to remember it but my memory card must be full. So it's the spontaneous joke, the remark in a circle of friends where there is history, trust and transparency that makes me laugh.

My antennae are always up for stuff that's cute, light, and humorous. I don't take myself that seriously anymore, and that's good advice at any age. People love honest self-deprecation. Can you make yourself the butt of a joke, rather than aiming the punch line at someone else, who may neither get it nor appreciate it? Making yourself the butt of your own joke makes you human and approachable. It shows you have your own concerns and problems: You get heartburn, suffer the heartbreak of psoriasis, don't know the difference between a five iron and a three wood, get caught stealing the last cookie, run out of gas on your way to your own party. Whatever it is, when you put yourself on the short end of your own story, you reveal your humanity, and people like it.

I'll tell you something that really helped me understand humor, the intoxicating power of audience laughter and the awful humility that can come when you lay yourself out on stage like a pork loin beneath a butcher's cleaver.

About 10 years ago, I decided to do something dramatic to break out of my comfort zone and dive into a totally foreign endeavor. I wanted to strip my veneer of position, grind away my self-perception of dignity, and stand naked and transparent on a stage that could either humiliate me or transport me beyond the comedic cosmos directly to humor heaven.

I took six weeks of improvisation training and performed at a comedy club in Raleigh.

For six weeks, my small group of courageous conquistadors worked with some improv actors who tried to tell us how to take a suggested scenario, mull it over for a moment, then mine it mirthfully and mercilessly for verbal and physical jokes before a live audience. We each had one minute to nail it—or die. I died a thousand deaths, and that was just the first week.

★

Maybe you're a Swiss psychiatrist engaged to treat a psychotic kangaroo. Take it from there.

The audience was live—at least before I started. Each second ticked like a Chinese gong as I racked my brain for inspiration. It's a minute that lasts a month.

Several people in my group dropped out. They just couldn't do it. The pressure, the transparency, the vulnerability was too much for them. I stuck it out, sweated through a shirt each show and earned a few laughs. I learned a lot about my limits and discovered they were nowhere near as close to me as I'd thought.

Knowing my position with Baptist Children's Homes and as a minister, which to him translates "humorless," the instructor at first was reluctant to let me take the stage after our initial session. I begged. He relented, and I "performed" each week.

At the end, he came to me, hand out, smile on his face. I thought he was going to offer me a gig in Los Angeles. Instead, he said, "You know my advice to you? Keep your day job."

The experience did wonders for me in subduing a lot of inhibitions. The setups were so absurd, but the absurd is a goldmine of giggles. They forced me to get out of my little box: I realized I'm too confined.

Stepping onto that stage not knowing where I'm going forced me to be instantly creative then and freed me to be more spontaneous when I speak now.

★

I use fewer notes and am more confident thinking on my feet.

One of the dangers of looking for the humor in things is that as a society we've become hypersensitive and politically correct. I'm not in favor of demeaning an ethnic group for a laugh; or making fun of a handicap, or shortcoming. We can be funny and stay above base humor. But even the most innocuous comment can ignite a social media firestorm. That's why I don't do social media. I know I could extend my "brand" through Twitter and Facebook but it's not worth the risk of being misinterpreted, misquoted, and brutalized for an insult I never intended.

Susan Sparks, a minister, lawyer, and comedian in New York City, calls laughter "the GPS for the soul" and says the ancients honored laughter as a spiritual healing tool.

"So why aren't we laughing along the spiritual path today?" she asks. She calls worship time in church "the dour hour" because we seem to think a long face is the only proper demeanor during that time.

She wrote **Laugh Your Way to Grace: Reclaiming the Spiritual Power of Humor** to help us understand that the power of humor radiates far beyond punch lines. Laughter can help you:

- Debunk the myths that you don't deserve joy
- Find perspective when faced with adversity

⭐

- Exercise forgiveness for yourself and others
- Reclaim play as a spiritual practice
- Heal — emotionally, physically and spiritually
- Keep your faith when God is silent
- Live with elegance, beauty and generosity
of spirit

I said I don't remember jokes very well, and
I don't. But here are a few I like that can be good
learning ground. If you share this with your kids
and they ask, "Why is that funny?" you can explain it
to them and they'll start to see how humor permeates
everyday life.

Such as: I don't want to brag or make anyone
jealous, but I can still fit into the socks I wore in high
school.

"Why is that funny?" Explain that making
someone jealous implies the ability to have or do
something no one else can do. But everyone can still
fit into the socks they wore in high school because
feet don't grow, even if you add 100 pounds to your
body weight.

Or this: A man was sitting reading his newspaper when his wife hit him over the head with a frying
pan.

"What was that for?" the man asked.

"That was for the piece of paper with the name
Betty on it that I found in your trouser pocket," she
said.

The man told her "Betty" was the name of the

★

horse he bet on at the races last week.

The wife apologized and went on with her chores.

Three days later the man is watching TV when his wife walks in and bashes him on the head with an even bigger frying pan.

When he regains consciousness, he asked why she hit him again.

Wife replied, "Your horse just phoned!"

Or this one: Some retired guys were playing poker in their Florida condo clubhouse. Guido loses $500 on a single hand, clutches his chest and drops over dead.

The men look at each other, and finally Giovanni asks, "So, who's gonna tell his wife?"

Nobody volunteers, so they cut the cards to choose the messenger. Pasquale picks the low card and has to carry the bad news.

They tell him to be discreet, be gentle, don't make a bad situation any worse. "Discreet?" he says. "I'm the most discreet person you'll ever meet. Discretion is my middle name. Leave it to me!"

So, Pasquale goes over to Guido's condo and knocks on the door. The wife answers through the door and asks what he wants.

Pasquale declares, "Your husband just lost $500 in a poker game and is afraid to come home."

"Tell him to drop dead!" yells the wife.

"I'll go tell him," says Pasquale.

★

Finally: A reporter interviewing a 104-year-old woman asks, "What do you think is the best thing about being 104?" She simply replies, "No peer pressure."

Your children are dealing with the constant pressure from kids their age to be, dress, act, slouch, and be digitally connected in a certain way. This woman has no one her age to pressure her into anything!

Each of these stories requires a certain bit of worldly knowledge and experience before the listener understands why they're funny. Eventually, you can get tuned in to the conversation, puns, plays on words, surprise endings to a long story to see the humor in them. When you can do that, you'll wear a smile so often that people will wonder what you're up to.

Keep them guessing.

SECURITY

No. 7

Finding freedom and confidence
in a well-planned future

★

CHAPTER 7

Planning for the Storm

What are you working toward?

What motivates you to obey the alarm clock and go through your morning routine in preparation to leave the house? Why do you go to work?

Obviously, we all need to earn money to pay the bills. But if your work is only a penance you pay so you can meet your obligations, is it bringing you the happiness you deserve? If you're not happy at work, much of your life is affected by that unhappiness.

So why do you do it?

Ultimately, we work—and identify with the work we do—because we want security. We don't want to worry that the bank is going to reclaim the car, that we're going to lose the house, or that our children might go to bed hungry.

We do this all of our lives, because we want to be sure that when we can no longer work we will still be able to have the resources necessary to stay safe

★

and secure in those areas. I get that.

Security (Safety) is the second level in American psychologist Abraham Maslow's hierarchy of needs, right above physiological needs. In other words, after we meet our immediate requirement for food and someplace to stay out of the rain, our very next concern as humans is security.

In earlier days, that meant finding a cave deep enough that a T. rex couldn't cram his little arms into it and snatch us out. Our ancestors wanted to know they could restart their fire if rain drenched it, and they wanted to have enough offspring that some would survive to carry on the tribe.

Former President Dwight D. Eisenhower understood security. He helped secure the world from the scourge of Nazi Germany. Even after that was done, though, he said, "If you want total security, go to prison. There you're fed, clothed, given medical care, and so on. The only thing lacking. . .is freedom."

On the other hand, Jon Krakauer, who writes real-life adventure books, including **Into the Wild** and **Into Thin Air**, suggests that security is the last thing a person needs to seek if that person wants to fully experience and enjoy life.

"So many people live within unhappy circum-stances and yet will not take the initiative to change their situation because they are conditioned to a life of security, conformity, and conservation, all of which may appear to give one peace of mind, but in reality

★

nothing is more damaging to the adventurous spirit within a man than a secure future," Krakauer wrote in **Into the Wild**. "The very basic core of a man's living spirit is his passion for adventure. The joy of life comes from our encounters with new experiences, and hence there is no greater joy than to have an endlessly changing horizon, for each day to have a new and different sun.

"If you want to get more out of life, you must lose your inclination for monotonous security and adopt a helter-skelter style of life that will at first appear to you to be crazy. But once you become accustomed to such a life, you will see its full meaning and its incredible beauty."

A recipe for adventure, maybe, but not a formula that most of us can follow.

I'm still working because I love to work and I love the work I do. I planned ahead so I could stop working eventually with the typical security that a well-planned retirement will provide. Because I love what I do, work is not a burden — it is my joy and my identity. I've not decided for sure, but I may be among the 10 percent of senior adults (did I just write "senior adults" in connection with my name?) who do not plan to retire at all.

What is security in this age, in this life?

I define security as your ability to live in the world confident that you've done everything necessary to assure that you can meet and provide for any

★

need that arises in your family as long as you live.

Unlike Eisenhower's observation about prison, in this kind of security comes freedom. What freedom do you really have if the specter of poverty or of living out your final years coughing and sleepless in a single room dangles over your head?

Krakauer's observation assumes there is no joy in working to provide that kind of security for your family. When your family is secure, you are free—free to explore, to risk, to retire, to try something new, to launch an adventure.

This kind of freedom does not come without planning.

Because my early jobs paid very little, and because starting a family ate up every nickel, I didn't start saving for retirement until I was 32. I worked at a church that paid me little. Their small package included a sum above the stated salary for "benefits" that the personnel committee told me I could "Do with it what you want."

I used it to feed my family.

That's bad advice if you're in that situation. But what can you do? The crying need of the moment drowns out the sleeping need of the future.

We lived like this: The check came in. We paid the rent, fed the kids and waited for the next check to come in.

I found extra work when I could. I'd be guest preacher, lead a retreat or a Bible study series, write

★

an article. I remember once that my only money was a silent dime in my pocket. It didn't even have another coin to jingle against.

I was teaching a Bible class for which I was being paid, and I went to the class knowing I really needed payment that night so I could buy some groceries on the way home. It was a bad feeling. I never want that feeling again.

I didn't invest in a retirement plan until I was a full-time pastor. It was the first time I had a dollar that I could set free expecting to recapture it with dividends tomorrow.

As soon as you possibly can do so, you must.

According to a story in 2015 **US News and World Report**, two-thirds of Americans depend on Social Security for at least 50 percent of their retirement income. Considering how many retirees there are now, more than a third of them depend on Social Security for 90 percent or more of their income.

Worse yet, for one-fourth of the 38.5 million people drawing benefits from Social Security, that program was their only source of retirement income. The average retirement benefit is about $1,200 a month.

Social Security was never meant to be your retirement fund. It was started to keep old people who could no longer work from starving in their homes and to give them an ounce of dignity.

I've put the maximum allowed by agency rules

★

and the law into my retirement fund ever since I possibly could. I have it taken out from my paycheck so I never see it. The more you put in, the better off you are and the more secure you will be later in life. Learn to live without that money. Find pleasure in seeing your account grow.

Eventually as you grow in your career and in wisdom, put additional money aside in a savings account to carry you through emergencies.

When the floorboards are coming loose, you can depend on your own intuition, your own work. Security has to come as a mind-set of what you believe you can count on.

The economic crash of 2008 annihilated many assumptions. It proved that job security and carefully plotted career paths are false. It proved a lie the adage that no one can lose money in real estate. It put many aging adults who were depending on their saving and investments into precarious positions, suddenly earning virtually nothing on their savings.

Consequently, the pages on your own retirement planning calendar may flip a lot more quickly than you intend. Writing in July 2015 in the **Washington Post**, columnist Rodney Brooks said an Employee Benefit Research Institute survey found that 50 percent of retirees left their jobs earlier than they had planned.

In other words, circumstances worked against them to force their retirement ahead of schedule.

★

Maybe they were laid off too young to retire but too old to get a job paying what they were making. Ageism exists.

You need to be prepared. Here is Brooks' cautionary prep list gleaned from financial advisers and retirement experts he consulted:

- **Do a budget.** It's important to know where money is coming from and where it's going.
- **Make extra payments on your mortgage and car.** If you are 55 and worried about losing your job at 60, make additional mortgage payments. Try to pay off your house in seven years so that when you are without work, that biggest budget item is no longer a worry. Similarly, try to have your car paid off by the time you are at highest risk of being terminated.

The more debt you can shed, the better off you will be. If you currently have two incomes in your family, ask yourself where you would be if you suddenly had only one.

- **Boost your emergency savings.** Pay yourself first and try to build up six months of cash reserve. If you can contribute to a Roth IRA, do so. Principal dollars can be pulled out at any time after you reach 59.5, so it is a good emergency pool.
- **Have a plan.** One counselor had clients with a long-term plan to move to Arizona upon retirement, and then the husband suddenly lost

★

his job. They re-evaluated what Social Security would be, what their pension would provide, what the sale of their home would provide, and what their dream house in Arizona would cost. It turned out they could go right now. Because they had been planning for years, the sudden loss of his job did not derail their dreams.

• **Keep your skills current and your résumé up to date.** Stay active in your professional networks. You may also lower your expectations for salary and benefits if you do land another job. People over 50 separated from their jobs often find it nearly impossible to find similar jobs and salaries.

A friend recently lost her job at age 62. The out-placement counselor her company provided told her that at her age she shouldn't waste her time looking for a job online, and sending her résumé through cyber space.

"You will get a new job through connections you've made during your career," he told her. He was right, and she had new work within the week.

Nurture your connections. They can provide you security in a constantly shifting landscape.

It's easier now than ever to cultivate connections and relationships. We have email, FaceTime, Facebook, Twitter, and LinkedIn. Goodness, people carry a phone in their pockets that makes them accessible around the clock to anyone in the world!

★

Make it a habit to follow up a meeting with a note. Get contact information. Exchange business cards so that a note is logical. People know that connections count so you are not out there slogging alone.

Friends are safe harbors when storms blow. Even the friends of the biblical character Job sat by him during his worst troubles. Sure, they urged him to curse God and die, but at least they were there!

Remember, if you've climbed over them on the way up, you're going to drop by them on your way down.

Dangerous years

Healthy-lifestyles researcher Dan Buettner delivered a 2009 TED Talk on his findings among people in certain areas of the world who tend to live inordinately long, healthy lives. He said, "The two most dangerous years of your life are the year you're **born** and the year you **retire**."

The first one, you can understand. But, the year you retire?

Bear Bryant didn't want to retire as football coach in Alabama because he thought he would die if he did. His last game was a 21–15 victory over the University of Illinois in the 1982 Liberty Bowl in Memphis, TN. At the press conference following the game, a reporter asked Bryant what he would do in retirement. He replied "Probably croak in a week."

Four weeks later, at age 69, he had a heart

★

attack and died.

Buettner found several areas in the world—which he called Blue Zones—with the longest disability-free life expectancy. One was Okinawa, where people commonly live past 100 and are physically capable, fully alert and involved in the world around them. They garden, play with their great-great grandchildren, and when they die, it is generally quickly and in their sleep.

According to Craig Weller, writing about this in his blog for **Barefoot Fitness**, Okinawans don't have a word for retirement. Instead, they use the term *Ikigai* which roughly translated means "passion" or "reason for living."

While conducting their study, Buettner's group asked Okinawans, "What is your *Ikigai*?" Nearly all of them were able to answer immediately. Can you?

The *Ikigai* for a 102-year-old karate master was to teach his martial art. For a 100-year-old fisherman, it was to continue bringing fish back from the sea to his family three days per week. A 102-year-old woman's Ikigai was to spend time with her great-great-great granddaughter.

In addition to diet and staying active, their passion kept them alive. They had something to rise and shine for every day. And it wasn't necessarily what they would call their "work."

Safety and security? They find it in living prudently, eating well and following their passion.

★

Another Blue Zone is in California, where Seventh-day Adventists live in their own community. They worship together, eat a similar, plant-based diet, and gain a great sense of security in community. The church is that for many.

Why is the year you retire one of your two most dangerous years? I believe it's because people in our culture find their **Ikigai** in their work. If they don't have their work, they drift without a purpose. Do they **have** a purpose anymore?

A trustee of my organization asked me recently if I plan to be around as president for another five years. "I hope so," I told her. I feel good, but I'll be 79 then and it's hard to envision.

But her question really pierced my thoughts. She asked what would I do in retirement, since not being around in five years would indicate I was retired—I hope—and not dead.

What would I do if I retired? Who would I be? Where is my identity then?

I confess my job is both my security and my identity. My employees are my family, and I'm almost a father figure now. They are not "like" family—they are family.

I'm so comfortable now that I can do things I never would have thought of earlier.

I recently did a spontaneous rap during a statewide event with hundreds of children and staff. They went wild! I donned period clothing

★

and portrayed Captain William Lafayette Kennedy during an alumni homecoming. Another time, a few years ago, I took off my shoes and dangled my feet over the stage talking to staff as if we were sitting on a creek bank.

As long as I've been in my current role and as well as staff know me, they still don't know what to expect now that I have this freedom because of the security of my work and the self-identity I find in it.

Yet, every day, I learn of other friends and colleagues who are deemed no longer "a fit" by their supervisors, and in the afternoon they are out of a job that they went to eagerly in the morning.

So in this climate, your job should not be the source of your security and identity. You need to have some kind of security beyond your job when you retire.

Do you have an avocation? What do you love to do outside of work? Do you wait for 5 o'clock to come so you can race home and immerse yourself in your hobby?

I saw it in churches. Members would be constricted in menial jobs during the day, but in church and in their volunteer roles they were a powerhouse. Maybe it was leading a Scout troop, or driving for Meals on Wheels, or teaching Sunday school, or serving as a deacon, or in homebound ministry. They found an activity they loved and in which they excelled and for which they became known.

★

A lot more preparation for retirement is required than getting your savings accounts in order. When there is suddenly twice as much of you around the house, will you get on your spouse's nerves? Do you each have enough of an outside interest that will engage you so you can enjoy it, and then bring the vitality of your interest back to the common table?

When you and your spouse nurture that relationship, you each gain security because you know no little argument or problem is going to break up the foundation you've built and nurtured.

Daily Security

No discussion on safety and security can neglect the fraying of our sense of security as we move about in our communities. I don't know that we feel safe anymore.

This is not a homogenous nation. We're not of one mind like we were in the days of our Founding Fathers. There seems to be no one, common goal or perspective pulling us toward a united future.

We once had a sense of pride and considered ourselves brothers and sisters simply because we were all Americans. That's not true anymore. Now we tend to see ourselves not as a part of the larger American identity but as a tribal member of some small special interest group.

That special interest becomes our primary concern, and we work for the benefit of that special interest, even to the detriment of the larger community. Our deal comes first.

I will tell you, trying to secure benefits for our tribe to the detriment of the larger community will ultimately doom our tribe.

Can you see the future you want to live toward? Ultimately it's going to come right down to security. We want a future that is secure.

I want security. And I want to know that my life mattered, and that there's life after retirement and I can still make a difference when I'm done with the nine to five, even if it's just a difference in my community.

I want to be able to listen, relate, talk, laugh, participate, and just to enjoy where I am in life because I've earned this. I've earned the right to take it easy, to step away, to retire and to have the last chapter of my life go well.

You may not have your spouse at the end, but you still want the love of your family, your children and grandchildren. You will want to know you're loved and that your life matters to someone.

From my vantage point, it ends in this positive note only if you nail things down early. Remember that you run out of "eventuallys" a lot faster than you can imagine. All those things that you will do "eventually" become impossible for the theft of time and energy.

★

Experiencing the wonder
of the universe

★

CHAPTER 8

Standing on a Rock that Never Rolls

I have great news for you—God is loose!

From humankind's first spiritual yearnings and awareness that there is a great, organizing principle to the universe that we call God, we've tried to put this Ultimate Being into a box that can be identified, comprehended and bent to our will.

We've organized vast numbers of religions around God, each slightly different from the others, and then rushed to battle over the differences. We fight because the box into which one group wanted to confine God is bigger or smaller or differently shaped from that of another.

People understand God differently. But if they yearn for, seek and bow down to God, they are humbling themselves as the created before the Creator.

I believe that God loves us and has gone to the extraordinary measure of taking on human form so that we can actually relate to God despite our very

★

limited human capacity—and that His will is that all be saved.

In a 2007 interview on Robert Schuller's *Hour of Power* television show, Billy Graham, no doubt the most iconic evangelical in the last century, said this about people who are seeking God:

"Whether they come from the Muslim world, or the Buddhist world, or the Christian world, or the non-believing world, they are members of the body of Christ because they've been called by God. They may not even know the name of Jesus, but they know in their hearts that they need something that they don't have, and they turn to the only light that they have, and I think that they are saved, and that they're going to be with us in heaven."

Here's the thing: There are people recognized as spiritual human beings, even by those who would not describe themselves as spiritual. The Pope, by his election by a conclave of the College of Cardinals, is recognized as an international spiritual leader. The Dalai Lama is recognized as a spiritual human being because of the equanimity and pervasive personal peace that emanates from him. Billy Graham is a spiritual person in the traditional Christian sense and is extraordinarily charismatic.

As humans, we instinctively know we are more than our frail flesh. We have in common an urgency to be a part of something bigger, to be a part of the great, vast Whole. We're aware of a spiritual self that yearns for God – a God in whom we can find meaning.

Being spiritual also means maintaining a balance between duty, responsibility and personal meditative experiences in which you renew yourself and listen. If you don't use it you lose it. It's not enough to know about prayer, to read about prayer, to discuss prayer with your friends, and hear sermons about prayer. Only the act of prayer, the intentional communing with God, will accrue the benefits of prayer.

How else will you tune your dial to that Great Broadcast beyond you? And once you break through the clutter and begin to receive nudges static-free, you must lock in that frequency and preserve it by whatever means necessary: silence, prayer, meditation, mentorship, seminars, and conversations with wise and spiritual people.

If you're running the ridge, you won't stay above the tree line for long without a spiritual awareness and intention to find how you fit into God's larger purpose: You need to be a spiritual leader.

In the face of many other definitions – often conflicting – true religion as defined in the Bible is pretty simple:

Religion that God our Father accepts as pure and faultless is this: to look after orphans and widows in their distress and to keep oneself from being

★

polluted by the world. (James 1:27)

That's where I've come down. That's what I've carried out in my life. I'm so fortunate to have been able to find that sweet spot in life and career that so matches my heart and fits the biblical definition of pure religion.

Follow Your Star

Consider the well-known story of three men who followed a star, a star which itself has been the subject of a great deal of speculation. The three men, of course, are the wise men. The Star is the Star of Bethlehem.

The planets Jupiter and Saturn were in close conjunction at that time—the time of Jesus' birth. Halley's Comet was also visible during that year, and the Star of Bethlehem could possibly have been a comet. Or perhaps a nova (or exploding star) could have marked the spot of Jesus' birth.

At any rate, a group of wise men, or **magi**, set out to follow this big sky show. The popular view lists these men as kings and makes them three in number, although the Bible does neither. According to Armenian tradition, their names are Balthazar, Caspar and Melchior.

Rather than kings, chances are they were really Babylonian astrologers/priests who scanned the sky and who believed that a new brightness in the heavens indicated that some unique personality had entered the world.

★

These men deserve our attention because they were willing to follow their star. They followed it until it stood "over the place where the child was." (Matthew 1:9)

For us, two millennia later, the star they followed represents vision — that moment of illumination that ignites our imagination and fires our will. Many people have trouble with life because they have never followed a star. They have never stood in the presence of a grand vision that gives meaning to their years.

Part of my father's family settled in the coal mining country of Kentucky. When I was a boy, I visited several mines with my uncle. I remember very vividly telling him there was no way that I could ever go into a dark tunnel to pick coal.

He simply knelt and picked up a piece of coal and said to me, "Son, I don't think you quite understand. This is not just a lump of coal. This is light and heat and power. Maybe it will light a city street or warm a home or run a train. I'm not just a coal miner. I'm the helper of people who never heard of me."

This is a vision. Every one of us can follow a star.

Years come and go. I cannot think of any quality more needed for facing another year than following a star. We humans mark the passing of time cyclically — a year is one pass of Earth around our sun.

★

You probably have some years that were so tough that you'd like to forget them.

The problem with that, of course, is that each year carries the baggage of the year before. But, each year also carries forward the wisdom gained so that we might make better choices as we journey on.

Ours is an uncertain time in an unfocused culture that lurches from crisis to crisis. We can't know the future except as the logical outgrowth—and dare I say repetition—of past events.

There is available to all a source of confidence that makes the angst of bad history and the trepidation of negative prognostications irrelevant. That source of confidence dwells in a God of hope, and that's about the most important four-letter word around right now.

Spiritual faith has always abounded in hope and expectation and promise for life. Through the centuries, nothing has been more characteristic of Christian people than a hope that enabled them to cope with life—a power to challenge and overcome circumstances instead of being devastated and overcome by them.

Out of a vast sky arrayed with stars, a spiritual leader chooses one to follow. For a Christian, the guiding star is Jesus Christ. When that Star commands our hearts, it draws us out of the basements of fear and resets us on the rooftops of hope to brave the blitz and bombs that would undo us.

★

A spiritual leader is focused on a star, and cannot truly lead without a deep awareness and appreciation for the spiritual.

Growing up, I appropriated as much as I understood of a spiritual self at an early age. I continue to appropriate it, even as I mature and as I know God and God makes Himself known more to me.

I've learned that God speaks more in silence than in much pleading.

Be quiet. I must insulate myself from all the noises around me so I can hear a word from God.

But when I am attentive and truly seeking direction, a word, or insight into a problem, I feel a nudge in my spirit. That nudge, when nurtured with prayer and contemplation, becomes the kernel that grows into a green stalk of truth from which I move and develop the truth as has been shown to me.

Truth with a capital "T" is always spiritual truth, by which you can live and move and have your being. It's the point from which I start and end, and the point from which I will not be moved. I must declare, as Martin Luther reportedly did before the Holy Roman Emperor Charles V in 1521, "Here I stand; I can do no other."

But, how do you get to this point?

It is a quest and it just never stops. I continue to learn and be open and am aware. I've learned to listen and remain open to whatever is around me: a child giving a testimony, a group singing; hearing the

★

trauma of a child who has overcome adversity and who in her own way proclaims that her victory is because of God's presence in her life.

Children in care at Baptist Children's Homes do not score high initially on the hope scale. They've all taken the train of trauma to get to us. Many have been sexually abused. To see them stand tall again—like Paulina, a precious young lady who was in our care—and relate in a large public forum how a houseparent led her to the Lord never ceases to thrill me. For her it was a religious experience.

Religious experiences and practice in the culture are being continually redefined.

Things just change.

Think of businesses that used to be closed on Sundays. Centuries before our blue laws, Jewish rules prohibited walking more than a quarter mile on the Sabbath, or even cooking. Now, we even have stores open on Christmas.

When I was a kid, we didn't go to movies on Sunday. Kids' athletic leagues wouldn't dare schedule a game on Sunday. You'd better get all the groceries you needed for Sunday lunch by Saturday or you would do without.

When I worked at WGNC radio during my high school years in Gastonia, North Carolina, we ran no advertising on Sunday. The owner, Mr. Todd, bequeathed it that way. It was his personal commitment to honor the Sabbath-keeping commandment.

★

When Sunday is just another day, it makes it that much harder for individuals in our culture to reclaim their sense of spirituality. In the midst of media bombardment and calendar tyranny, it is hard to make a space to touch base with our spiritual selves and the Spirit of God.

Where do we find a stream in the midst of this desert? Where do we find a spring to keep us going? Where do we find those moments?

You have to hunt for, discover, and then selfishly claim whatever those moments are for you.

You don't have to travel thousands of miles and gaze over the depths and chasms of the Grand Canyon to recognize the majesty of God. You don't have to climb Mt. Everest or cross an ocean.

If you will just intentionally carve quiet moments, shut out the din, assume a comfortable posture and listen, God will nudge you.

My wish for you is that you be a spiritual person. You can be a spiritual leader only if you are a spiritual person. I'm not talking about transforming your place of business into a monastery, convent or temple.

I find I cannot be fully human without being fully in touch with the inner spirituality with which God has endowed me.

People in tune with that spirit enjoy life despite negative physical circumstances. How do some, living in abject poverty, not despair? From whence can come

★

a positive word in a hospice bed? How is the grieving widow able to move into tomorrow?

They have found a way; they've done what it takes to connect their human spirit to the creative spirit.

Would you have a better life, a more spiritual and fulfilling life? Then do the work to discover your passion and find significance. Once you discover it, ride the wave.

What you want is a relationship with God. Here are some basic steps:

1. Listen.

2. Reflect on what you hear.

3. Ask, "What do I need to do?" My ethical question is not "What would Jesus do?" My ethical question is "What would Jesus have me do?"

4. Take action. When you hear a nudging answer, you are empowered and commissioned to do it. You have to execute, move out and do it. Or else the revelation just sits there.

Be the best pipefitter you can be, or the best garbage collector, schoolteacher, doctor or community leader.

I'm not cut out to tote and lug the garbage cans that stronger men can do day after day. But I appreciate their work, and at least once a year I make it a point to meet them at the end of my driveway and tell them so. Last summer, one of them told me, "I love what I do. I get to help people."

As I've released more of my own spirit through my life, I've grown more generous with my time, money and presence. That's the main thing I can give to people now: I give them me.

In return, I'm blessed with more opportunities to directly relate to other people. It seems people perceive that I'm more accessible now, and people who need to connect with me somehow do. They see in me someone who will listen, comfort, advise, and bless.

Recently at the YMCA, a widower poured out his grieving heart; two babies held out their arms and a little one came running up to me, a total stranger. "He never goes to anyone," said his trailing mother. I like that. There is something about my spiritual confidence on the ridge that encourages that.

I try to fill my thoughts with positive things and I believe that living in the spirit of gratitude is the key to happiness. It's a key to the whole process of developing your spirituality.

Your attitude is more important than your mental capacity when it comes to developing your spirit. The Apostle Paul wrote, "I have learned to be content in whatever circumstances I am." (Philippians 4:11)

I love the story about the 112-year-old North Carolina woman, Sina Hayes (she died in January 2016), who said the secret to her longevity is "happy thoughts." Her 90-year-old son, Carlyle, who called

★

her every day from Texas and came to see her four times a year, would say the same thing. He still works 15 hours a week, by the way.

When you allow the Spirit to shine through you, and release it to soften your countenance, and you become approachable, you become a resource for helping.

The organization of which I took the helm as a 41-year-old in no way today resembles what it was then. We are an institution of a large denominational organization that has known significant strife during my tenure. Yet, because of my longevity and growth, I've become a known and trusted leader. Part of my spirituality—my spiritual mission—is to say, "Come now, and let us reason together." (Isaiah 1:18)

LEGACY

No. 9

The script you are writing on the pages of history

★

CHAPTER 9

Accelerating Past the Finish Line

As he neared the end of his career, John Claypool, one of the best preachers ever grown in the Baptist garden, said the day eventually comes to each of us when we realize we have more sunsets than sunrises in our future.

While that doesn't make any sense when you know each day has both a sunrise and a sunset, the sentiment is true. You reach a point when you realize that you'd better wrap up your projects. The time for starting new things is growing short.

The curtain is dropping on your play and you're not getting cast in a new production.

It's the time when thoughts of your mortality creep in and you consider what you're leaving behind. You wonder how you'll be remembered. You think about your legacy.

Every day giants pass from the earth.

They leave this life — sometimes suddenly —

★

and we analyze their impact on art, music, industry, education, sports, government, and social service.

Or they finish a career, slip a gold watch onto their wrist and then read with others the reviews about how they influenced the way we live our lives. Former President George W. Bush said he will "leave it to history" to sort out his presidency. However, no one really serves in the Oval Office without one eye constantly turned toward legacy.

A key theme of many popular books and movies features someone's body of work that defines how we remember that person. At least three movies have been made about the life of Steve Jobs. Jobs is one of the founders of technology innovator Apple.

Consider volumes on Lincoln, Churchill, Kennedy, and every military and political world leader whose decisions changed the course of world events as if they were a large rock dropped suddenly in a local fishing pond.

These definitive biographies are written after the subject's death—their legacy in the hands of others, to evaluate, interpret, and define.

Glenn Frey, lead singer and primary song writer for The Eagles—a band that created the West Coast, rock/country sound that dominated the 1970s— died in 2016. One of his last songs indicated that he was thinking about legacy in his final days. Some poignant words in "It's Your World Now" go like this:

★

". . .I must be leavin' soon
It's your world now. . .
My race is run
I'm moving on. . .
It's your world now
Use well the time
Be part of something good
Leave something good behind
The curtain falls
I take my bow
That's how it's meant to be
It's your world now."

Christian singer Nicole Nordeman asks in **Legacy**, "How will they remember me? Did I choose to love? Did I point to You enough to make a mark on things? I want to leave an offering, a child of mercy and grace who blessed Your name unapologetically, and leave that kind of legacy."

If you are running the ridge above the tree line, if you are thriving at the peak of your career and in family and spiritual life, you've probably thought about your legacy for some years. If not, consider that building your legacy starts within the context of the life you're living right now.

Should you care about your legacy? Of course. First, understand that you will leave a legacy, whether or not you're conscious of establishing it. That is, unless you were born in isolation and raised by wild animals like Romulus and Remus of ancient

Roman myth, or like Rudyard Kipling's Mowgli from *The Jungle Book*. On second thought, I guess they DID leave a legacy, since we have their stories! So, there's no escaping it.

Secondly, you can, like many highly-accomplished men and women who have gone before you, live distinctly aware that you are growing a legacy—for good or ill, for a day or a century—and consciously live to leave the world a better place for your having been an occupant.

In the early 1700s in Colonial America, a husband's and wife's devotion to each other and to their faith established a legacy far beyond what most of us can imagine. Their names were Jonathan and Sarah Edwards.

Jonathan Edwards was pastor of a small New England congregation. During his tenure, he wrote many sermons, prayers and books that became influential in sparking the Great Awakening.

They included their 11 children in family conversations and decision making. The effects of the Edwardses' lives have been far-reaching, but the most measurable result of their faithfulness to God's call is found through their descendants. A study done by A.E. Winship in 1900 lists a few of the accomplishments of the 1,400 Edwards descendants he was able to find:

- 100 lawyers and a dean of a law school
- 80 holders of public office
- 66 physicians and a dean of a medical school

★

- 65 professors of colleges and universities
- 30 judges
- 13 college presidents
- 3 mayors of large cities
- 3 governors of states
- 3 United States senators
- 1 controller of the United States Treasury
- 1 Vice President of the United States

This evaluation of Jonathan and Sarah Edwards makes much of career and professional position to measure legacy, but legacy is so much broader. Your legacy of faithfulness to your spouse, to your family and religion, to your work and friends is every bit as valid a measure. Faithfulness begets faithfulness. Trust begets trust. Loving parents beget loving children—not always, of course, but more often than not.

Your life matters. Your life is a legacy. Live like it.

Your legacy is the script you're writing on the pages of history; the difference you make that at some point in someone's life will prompt a memory of you. You want it to be positive, but not all legacies are, of course. Many historical figures are remembered for their horrendously negative legacies: Hitler, Stalin, Mussolini, and Lee Harvey Oswald.

How do you leave a positive legacy? Ask yourself, "What can I do to make life better for others?"

I try to be a realist. I've been a radio DJ, a newspaper journalist, a television anchor, a youth minister and pastor of churches. I'm a father, husband, grandfather, friend. I'm a "guy at the Y" for some. For others, I'm an author, speaker, neighbor, boss, and counselor. So what will be my legacy?

I think my legacy started to take shape in 1970 at Ridge Road Baptist Church in Raleigh, NC where I was minister to youth and college students. I have a legacy there that is regularly renewed because I stay in touch with many of the "kids" — now senior adults — who were college students when I was their minister. One of them is an executive with CNN, and when his mother and father died within a few weeks of each other, I called him to express my love and concern and to share memories.

"You'll never know what this call meant," he told me. "When I was in your youth group, it was the first time in my life that I felt like 'somebody.' Your affirmation and belief in me will always be part of my life."

My body of work has established me as a person of positive influence in others' lives.

I say that in all humility because this really is the first time in my life that this only child, who was blessed with a resonant voice, a tender heart, and a strong mind, has realized that people look up to me just because of who I am. You'd think I would have more self-confidence than that, that I would have shouldered the public perception of "president" and expected people to respond to the position and to me

★

as the one who holds it.

But, no. It took decades of hard work, a trail of successes, a consistent life, and faithful service to reach that point. And I'm only just realizing it from my view on the ridge.

Musician David Bowie died in 2016. The extent of his work pushed him always to the front edge of music innovation. He was ill with cancer, but no one knew it. He put out a new record over the final weekend of his life. He was aware of his legacy and honored it as much as he could until the end.

I imagine that whoever defines my legacy for the next generation will focus on my work as president of Baptist Children's Homes of North Carolina. I'm only the second president in the past 58 years. BCH has had eight presidents in a history that began in 1885.

For sure, I will leave a legacy. I'm aware that I don't control the interpretation of that legacy. For certain, I want it to be positive.

In the second **Back to the Future** movie, Bif controlled the economy because he had information from a book he'd recovered from the future that had the results of every competition — from horse racing, to football games. He bet big and never lost.

Because Bif had no conscience, he felt no compulsion to build positively on what others had built before him. There will be a legacy. In Bif's case, it will be one of having destroyed what was good out of

★

greed and selfishness.

My parents cared enough to teach me principles that kept me from being a Bif, like an electric-shock collar keeps a dog in his own yard. I'm not going to steal or cheat. My upbringing provided a moral compass that says, "It is not honorable to go beyond this point."

I always felt that I don't want to do anything that would spoil my parents' confidence in me.

Of course, people sometimes get off track. But you have to come back, re-center yourself. Commit to doing right and to being the person you intend to be. If you wonder whether an action or opportunity is right or wrong, it's probably wrong.

I intentionally avoid like the plague any hint of scandal. I don't even know how to get into our company's post office box or the safe in the business office. I have no need to know.

I am uncomfortable when people give me cash money as a gift for Baptist Children's Homes. One time a guy shoved four one-hundred dollar bills into my hand after I'd spoken in his church. Those bills burned a hole in my pocket all the way home until I could get them processed through our accounting department.

To claim any such gifts for myself has never been a temptation. I never had the internal conversation that "no one will know if I just use that money for myself."

★

It would haunt me. You just can't yield.

I already deal with enough guilt from my short-comings as a son, as a parent, as a friend. What could I have done better for my kids? How could I have been a better parent and husband? How could I have been more compassionate when slings and arrows opened wounds in my children or friends?

Be true to yourself. Be true to your values. Life is compromise but you must maintain a point beyond which you will not go. If you have to be dishonest to gain a contract, let the contract go. Others will come along.

Once you start down that slippery slope, it's easy to justify doing it again, and operating that way could work itself into your mind and taint your legacy.

I've continued the vision that our founder John Mills cast. He left an incredible legacy and I've treated it as a precious jewel, polishing it and keeping it safe. There will be a legacy!

To that end, I've been asking myself certain questions to focus my work in my remaining career years.

- Did I put into place a method of operation that will endure and continue to give opportunity to all residents to achieve their dreams?
- Will I leave behind an institution that has moved beyond custodial care to tap the creative genius that lies in the bosom of every child?

★

• Have I inspired other people to dedicate themselves to achieving things of lasting value that will live into succeeding generations?

• Have I put into place a "culture of excellence" rooted deeply enough that new staff and new leadership will be committed to replicate and expand its successes?

• Have I cultivated new donors and secured their commitment to BCH's ongoing success and financial vitality?

People tend to think about legacy in the final years of their career. That's too late because you started laying bricks on the house of your legacy years ago. You started building your career legacy when you started your career.

I know that is true; however, I just started actually considering my legacy in the past year—truly. Until then I've just worked at the task before me, doing my job, giving it my best shot, remaining open to the Spirit, willing to take risks, seeking to be creative, measuring the costs. Then, at a certain point, I realized that my stamp is going to be on this place for a good while.

Young ridge runners, ask yourselves now: "What do I want to build?" Don't let your legacy be built on the random accumulation of acts and facts, plum and glum jobs, successes and digresses that your career will naturally take.

What do you want to do with yourself? What

★

do you want to accomplish? What dried footprint in the muddy bottom of time do you want to leave? Yes, when all is said and done, how do you want to be remembered?

Success is more than just showing up. Your legacy is built like success is built—by doing the next thing well, and with passion and inspired creativity.

American philosopher William James said, "The great use of a life is to spend it for something that outlasts us."

Your legacy is the record of things that outlast you. I'm serious when I say it's more than career.

When television journalist Matt Lauer asked President Obama about his legacy, he said, "Ultimately, how well you've done here is going to be judged not by tomorrow's polls or today's headlines. You're going to be judged by people who are looking back at you 20-30 years from now, and so you'd better let'er rip."

President Obama's predecessor, George W. Bush, took a more detached approach to the same question when he said, "I'm going to be dead when my legacy is decided."

Muhammad Ali, who died June 4, 2016, was never shy about how he hoped his legacy would endure: *I would like to be remembered as a man who won the heavyweight title three times, who was humorous, and who treated everyone right. As a man who never looked down on those who looked up to*

★

him, and who helped as many people as he could. As a man who stood up for his beliefs no matter what. As a man who tried to unite all humankind through faith and love. And if all that's too much, then I guess I'd settle for being remembered only as a great boxer who became a leader and champion of his people. And I wouldn't even mind if folks forgot how pretty I was.

It's not vanity to think about your legacy. It's vanity to think that every decision and move you make has to be legacy-oriented resulting in not doing anything of any consequence.

Someone consciously building a legacy may start to order events around himself/herself. I've found in my "legacy-conscious" period that the opposite is occurring. I'm in a position to step off center stage and let the spotlight illuminate those we serve, rather than me.

On a recent Sunday, Baptist Children's Homes brought a large group of our residents to present at a local Baptist church. I try to stay out of the way and let the children's smiles and tears tell their story.

As emcee, I have to be attentive to the moment. One little 5-year-old boy in our care never took his eyes off me. I asked him to give me a high five, and he came running down. His name is Ethan and he looks just like Ralphie from the perennial *A Christmas Story* movie.

I started to interview him and he's like a 35-

year-old.

"What do you want to be when you grow up?"

"I want to be a weatherman."

We talked, and he captivated the entire congregation. They were enthralled, and Ethan ate it up, responding to their vocal encouragement with growing confidence and cuter responses.

When church members recall this incident, what they are going to remember is that Ethan stole the show.

They won't consider that I was attuned to the Spirit in the moment, or that three other kids who spoke told me they loved me and gave me big hugs on the stage. And that is all fine with me because at this stage my legacy is not about me personally, but about what I've left behind.

In fact, I received a note from a board member after that church presentation, which expressed gratitude for the wonderful, inspirational service and said, "The children led us." That confirmed my intention to step back, be Spirit-led, and let the children speak.

These children are my legacy. When I consider that I've had a hand in solidifying an organization that will function for another century helping children who hurt and healing broken families, I can lay my head down at night and sleep blissfully.

Twenty years ago, I asked one of our former residents who has a beautiful singing voice and a transparent heart to speak to several churches

★

during our fall emphasis. Roberta did a magnificent job and has continued to help us, representing the best of our work.

She was speaking on this same Sunday and just before her presentation, I mentioned that I knew it would be a hard day for her because it was the anniversary of her mother's death one year earlier.

Her mother had been cruel to her, but late in her life she had accepted Roberta's forgiveness and accepted the forgiveness that Jesus offers and had become a Christian. That meant the world to Roberta.

It meant the world to her that I remembered the anniversary of her mother's death and committed to pray her through the tough anniversary. My legacy will live in Roberta's retelling of that story. It's not about my being on stage, it's about the kernel of transparency and influence sprouting in another's life and bursting forth in flowers and fruit.

Obeying your call to execute and exercise your gifts sets the parameters for the way people remember you.

I build my legacy now on tuning in to what I feel the Spirit is saying to me. Spontaneity is a new strength and a new way of operating for me. Neither my legacy nor my life is scripted anymore. I'm basing my life on moments. They're tiring. They're exhausting, but they're so much fun.

At age 75, world famous evangelist Billy Graham was asked how he wanted to be remembered.

★

Surprisingly—to me then, but not now—he said, "I want to be remembered as someone fun to live with."

For me, I want my grandchildren to remember me as a loving, devoted, funny grandpa. To them I'm not Dr. Blackwell, and they have no illusions about what I do or who will take my calls. I'm just "Boppy."

My kids will remember me in some way that was established while they were growing up, while I wrestled with career and expectations and professional pressures and had not arrived at my place above the tree line.

But I'm still forming my legacy with my grandchildren. Gabriella and Piper like that I can make them laugh, and making them laugh brings me joy.

If you are casting your thoughts forward to consider your legacy, think of this: Start out the way you want to end up.

I started out wanting to be the best newspaper reporter I could be. I had a very tough journalism professor in Walter Spearman. He was a great writer, brilliant, moody, a chain smoker (even in class), and the best punster I ever heard. When he was in a bad mood, he could stick a pin in any aspiring journalist's dream balloon and leave a deflated student to slink away in tears.

Because he was so hard, serious students wanted desperately to please him. A kind word, a back handed-compliment, a positive notation on

★

an assignment was like a surprise ice cream cone on a hot day.

So I worked hard to please Walter Spearman because I knew if I could make him happy, I would be on my way to achieving my goal of being an excellent reporter. One day after a particularly tough assignment, Spearman was railing at the class's general failure to come through for him.

For a moment I assumed I was lumped in with everyone else, and then he said, "Nobody in here would have ever gotten this story, except Mickey."

As a student of Walter Spearman's, that was the highest compliment I could get. While trying to stay humble, I must have been puffed up like a puffer fish. That might have been the day I started balding on top because my head got too big for my hair.

From the beginning of my conscious life, I wanted to be really good at whatever I did. I never wanted to be mediocre—ever—at anything. I've never lost that feeling, and I remain committed to it.

When I was the only first-grader invited to participate in the second grade talent show, I wanted to be the best. When I helped to change Charlotte radio at WAYS, I wanted to be the best news director on air.

I wanted to be the best journalist, the best youth minister, the best student in seminary, the best pastor, and certainly the best CEO of my organization. Do you see the common thread? Others will write of your legacy, but if you are going to give them something

★

positive to write about, it will be built only on the back of your best.

You can think, "This is how I want to be remembered." But others will interpret your life, career and contributions. If you've given less than your best, your legacy will be less than what you wish.

Just as I opened this chapter with the idea of there being more sunsets than sunrises in my future, I realize I have a limited time to clean projects off my plate and prepare the office for its next occupant. At the same time, I want to do "just a few more things" that have been lingering so BCH can be in the best shape possible for my successor.

I need to refresh the board of trustees: This is a wonderful board and a faithful board, but eight or nine of them are in their 80s. I need to find some new people who will be the kind of board members these folks have exemplified.

Can I get some non-Baptists involved? Our ministry serves children and families of every background and ethnicity. Baptists are not the only ones who love children and want to meet their needs. Our documents require trustees to be Baptist, but there may be other leadership groups I can get started to include non-Baptists.

It sounds like I have a lot yet to do and that's true. But, they're not going to have to carry me out of my office. I want to have two or three weeks of retirement before I die!

I want to end my tenure — in office and on earth — waving the checkered flag of victory. I want to cross the finish line still accelerating. I'll reach for the flag and take my victory lap with shouts of joy.

Who determines your legacy? Victors write the histories. This book is an intentional part of my legacy. I want it to be a tool, so I've shared nine chapters of life lessons. I hope readers will know the values upon which my legacy is built — however others interpret it.

The important thing to remember is that these are not values I adopted so that I could build a positive legacy. These are the values I adopted to live by, so that I could have a positive life.

That, ultimately, will be your legacy — the life you lived.

If it stands the tests of those who follow, then you have lived a good life. You will have left a fine legacy.

Just as Billy Graham's wish to be remembered as someone fun to live with may have surprised you, I confess that part of me would like to be remembered as a master communicator, as someone who can inspire and encourage through the written, spoken and preached word. An orator.

Orators who have made a difference over the centuries have said something important that never died. Communicating is my gift and I've used it to

★

build up BCH. I've used it to inspire trust in our mission, in our leadership and in me. That is vital to secure the commitments necessary to keep BCH thriving.

Throughout my life, wherever there is a microphone, a newspaper column, a challenge, a cause, a group gathered, a vacant pulpit, a convention, a seminar, or a television interview, I've considered it an opportunity to shine on behalf of my organization—and even my legacy.

Maybe that's why, when a reporter asked me to sum up my life in two words, I said, "Show Time."

Henry Scott-Holland, a priest at St. Paul's Cathedral in London, delivered this poem in 1910 as part of a eulogy for a parishioner. It may be Scott-Holland's legacy because it lives after him more than a century later.

I share it with you to close this chapter, and this book, because the very term "legacy" implies death. And death, as literary critic Northrop Frye reminds us, is "not the opposite of life but the opposite of birth." The one who has left a legacy to be remembered is no longer among us.

> *Death is nothing at all. It does not count.*
>
> *I have only slipped away into the next room.*
>
> *Nothing has happened. Everything remains exactly as it was.*
>
> *I am I, and you are you, and the old life that we lived so fondly together is untouched, unchanged.*

★

Whatever we were to each other, that we are still.

Call me by the old familiar name. Speak of me in the easy way which you always used.

Put no difference into your tone. Wear no forced air of solemnity or sorrow.

Laugh as we always laughed at the little jokes that we enjoyed together. Play, smile, think of me, pray for me.

Let my name be ever the household word that it always was. Let it be spoken without an effort, without the ghost of a shadow upon it.

Life means all that it ever meant. It is the same as it ever was. There is absolute and unbroken continuity.

What is this death but a negligible accident? Why should I be out of mind because I am out of sight?

I am but waiting for you, for an interval, somewhere very near, just around the corner.

GodSpeed

About the Author

Dr. Michael C. Blackwell has been president of Baptist Children's Homes of North Carolina since July 1983, turning it into an aggressive, active, growing center for innovation in 21 communities across the state, serving thousands of children and senior adults annually.

He has directed the formulation and implementation of strategic plans, the successful completion of three major capital campaigns, and the creation of public-private partnerships to better serve youth and families.

He is in demand as a motivational speaker and is the author of four previous books: **New Millennium Families** (2000), **A Place for Miracles** (2002), **UpsideDown Leadership** (2003), and **Riches Beyond Measure** (2004). Journalist Wint Capel wrote a biography on Blackwell entitled **Just Call Me Mickey: From Mill Village to Mills Home** published in 2006.

Blackwell is a native of Gastonia, NC, a journalism graduate of the University of North Carolina at Chapel Hill, a former newspaper reporter and radio and television news anchor. He is an ordained minister with

★

Master of Divinity, Master of Theology, and Doctor of Ministry degrees. Dr. Blackwell was awarded an honorary Doctor of Humane Letters degree from Campbell University in Buies Creek, NC, in 2003.

Dr. Blackwell leads the largest children's home network in the Southeast. During his 33-year presidency, BCH has expanded services to include weekday education, wilderness camping, a working ranch, and family care as well as ministry to adults with developmental disabilities. In 2009, Dr. Blackwell led BCH to begin a new, non-residential ministry called North Carolina Baptist Aging Ministry. In 2014, Baptist Children's Homes began an orphanage in Guatemala. In 2016, a new ministry to Western Carolina University students in Cullowhee, NC was launched. And in 2017, The Bob and Carolyn Tucker Greater Vision Ministry Center will become a reality.

The Baptist Children's Homes and its affiliated ministries serve more than 22,000 people annually.

★